2nd Edition

THE EASY CHRISTMAS FAKE BOOK

Melody, Lyrics and Simplified Chords

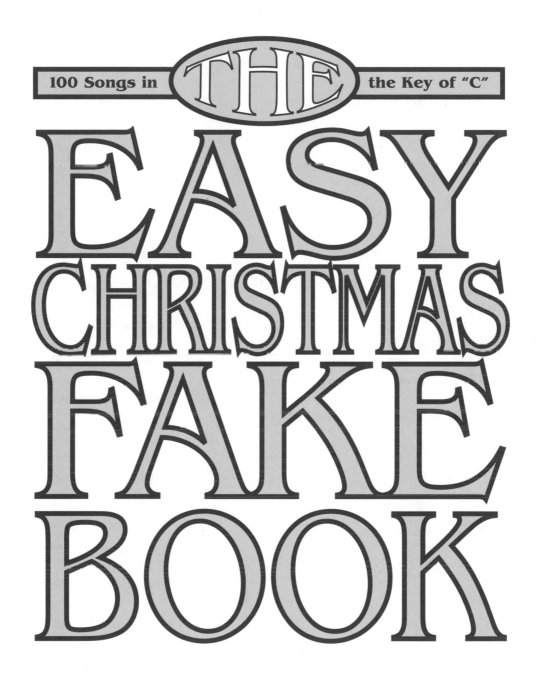

100 Songs in THE the Key of "C"

THE EASY CHRISTMAS FAKE BOOK

ISBN 978-0-634-04911-8

HAL•LEONARD® CORPORATION

7777 W. BLUEMOUND RD. P.O. BOX 13819 MILWAUKEE, WI 53213

Visit Hal Leonard Online at
www.halleonard.com

THE EASY CHRISTMAS FAKE BOOK

CONTENTS

INTRODUCTION

What Is a Fake Book?

A fake book has one-line music notation consisting of melody, lyrics and chord symbols. This lead sheet format is a "musical shorthand" which is an invaluable resource for all musicians—hobbyists to professionals.

Here's how *The Easy Christmas Fake Book* differs from most standard fake books:

- All songs are in the key of C.

- Many of the melodies have been simplified.

- Only five basic chord types are used—major, minor, seventh, diminished and augmented.

- The music notation is larger for ease of reading.

In the event that you haven't used chord symbols to create accompaniment, or your experience is limited, a chord speller chart is included at the back of the book to help you get started.

Have fun!

ALL I WANT FOR CHRISTMAS IS YOU

Words and Music by MARIAH CAREY
and WALTER AFANASIEFF

- mas day. __ I just want you for ___ my own, __
- deer click. __ I just want you here ___ to - night, __
___ my door. __ I just want him for ___ my own, __

more than you could ev - er know. __ Make my wish come true: __
hold - ing on to me ___ so tight. __ What more can I do? __
more than you could ev - er know. __ Make my wish come true: __

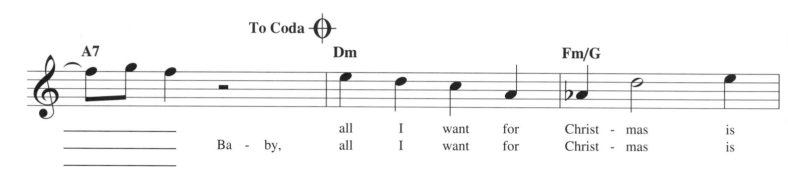

_____ ___
_____ Ba - by, all I want for Christ - mas is
_____

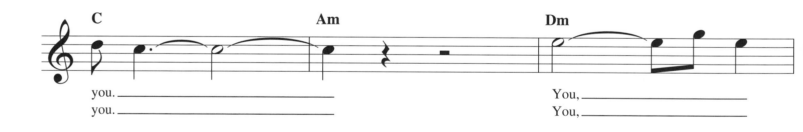

you. _____
you. _____ You, _____
You, _____

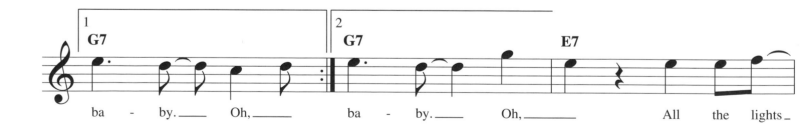

ba - by. __ Oh, __ ba - by. __ Oh, __ All the lights __

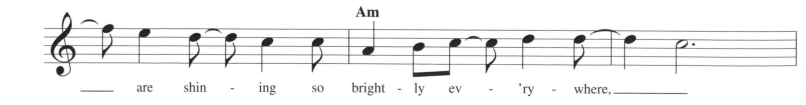

___ are shin - ing so bright - ly ev - 'ry - where, __

and the sound_____ of chil - dren's laugh - ter fills_____ the air._____

_____ And ev - 'ry - one_____ is sing - ing,

I hear those sleigh_____ bells ring - ing. San - ta, won't you please bring me

what I real - ly need? Won't you please bring my ba - by to me?_____ Oh,_____

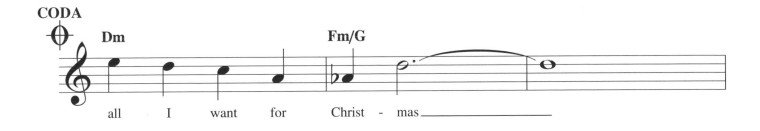

all I want for Christ - mas_____

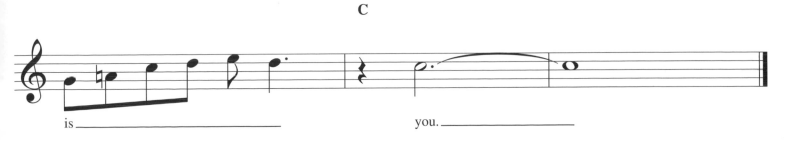

is_____ you._____

ANGELS FROM THE REALMS OF GLORY

Words by JAMES MONTGOMERY
Music by HENRY T. SMART

With spirit

An - gels from the realms of glo - ry, Wing your flight o'er
Shep - herds in the fields a - bid - ing, Watch - ing o'er your
Sag - es, leave your con - tem - pla - tions; Bright - er vi - sions
Saints be - fore the al - tar bend - ing, Watch - ing long in

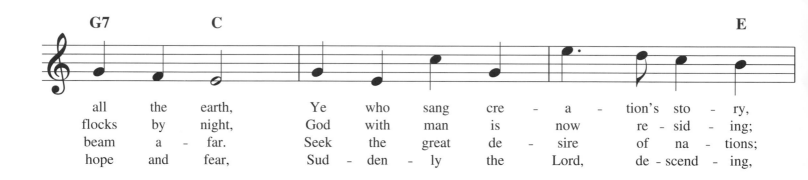

all the earth, Ye who sang cre - a - tion's sto - ry,
flocks by night, God with man is now re - sid - ing;
beam a - far. Seek the great de - sire of na - tions;
hope and fear, Sud - den - ly the Lord, de - scend - ing,

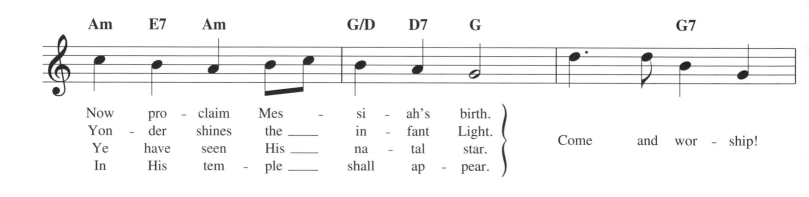

Now pro - claim Mes - si - ah's birth.
Yon - der shines the ___ in - fant Light.
Ye have seen His ___ na - tal star.
In His tem - ple ___ shall ap - pear.

Come and wor - ship!

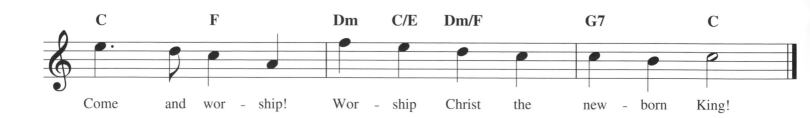

Come and wor - ship! Wor - ship Christ the new - born King!

ANGELS WE HAVE HEARD ON HIGH

Traditional French Carol
Translated by JAMES CHADWICK

AULD LANG SYNE

Words by ROBERT BURNS
Traditional Scottish Melody

Slowly

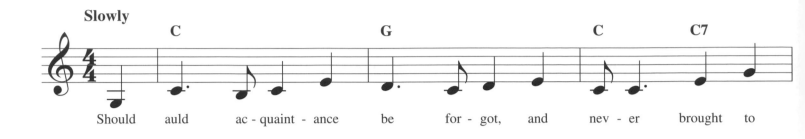

Should auld ac - quaint - ance be for - got, and nev - er brought to

mind? Should auld ac - quaint - ance be for - got and

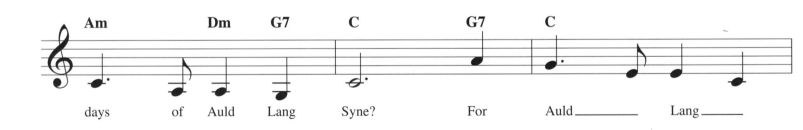

days of Auld Lang Syne? For Auld_____ Lang_____

Syne, my dear, for Auld_____ Lang_____ Syne, We'll tak' a cup o'

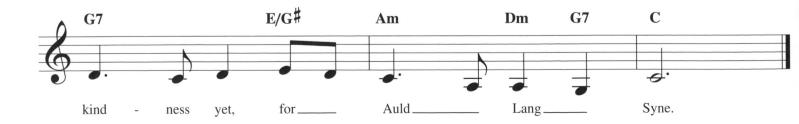

kind - ness yet, for_____ Auld_____ Lang_____ Syne.

AWAY IN A MANGER

Traditional
Words by JOHN T. McFARLAND (v.3)
Music by JAMES R. MURRAY

Tenderly

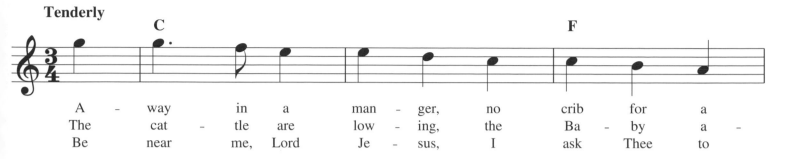

A - way in a man - ger, no crib for a
The cat - tle are low - ing, the Ba - by a -
Be near me, Lord Je - sus, I ask Thee to

bed, The lit - tle Lord Je - sus laid
wakes, But lit - tle Lord Je - sus no
stay Close by me for - ev - er, and

down his sweet head. The stars in the
cry - ing He makes. I love Thee, Lord
love me, I pray. Bless all the dear

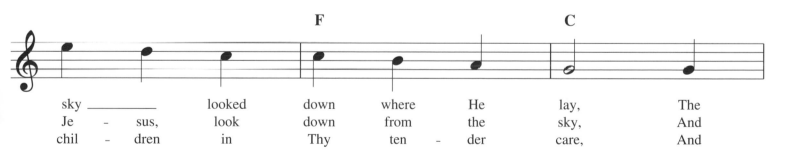

sky _____ looked down where He lay, The
Je - sus, look down from the sky, And
chil - dren in Thy ten - der care, And

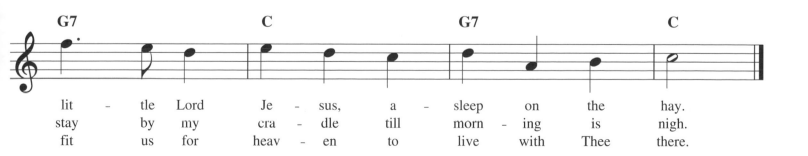

lit - tle Lord Je - sus, a - sleep on the hay.
stay by my cra - dle till morn - ing is nigh.
fit us for heav - en to live with Thee there.

BABY, IT'S COLD OUTSIDE
from the Motion Picture NEPTUNE'S DAUGHTER

By FRANK LOESSER

I real - ly can't stay, _____ I've got to go 'way. _____
sim - ply must go, _____ the an - swer is No! _____

___ This eve - ning has been _____ so ver - y nice. _____
___ The wel - come has been _____ so nice and warm. _____

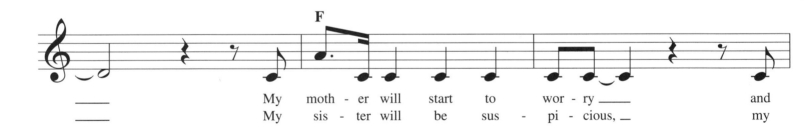

My moth - er will start to wor - ry _____ and
My sis - ter will be sus - pi - cious, ___ my

fa - ther will be pac - ing the floor. So real - ly I'd bet - ter
broth - er will be there at the door. My maid - en aunt's mind is

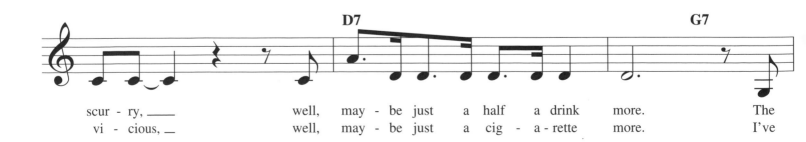

scur - ry, ___ well, may - be just a half a drink more. The
vi - cious, ___ well, may - be just a cig - a - rette more. I've

neigh - bors might think; _____ say, what's in this drink? _____
got to get home; _____ say, lend me a comb. _____

_____ I wish I knew how _____ to break the
_____ You've real - ly been grand _____ but don't you

spell. _____ I ought to say "No, no,
see. _____ There's bound to be talk to -

no, sir!" __ At least I'm gon - na say that I tried. I
mor - row. __ At least there will be plen - ty im - plied. I

real - ly can't stay _____ ah, but it's cold _____ out -
real - ly can't stay _____ ah, but it's cold _____ out -

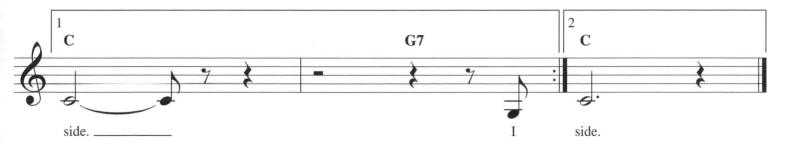

side. _____ I side.

BECAUSE IT'S CHRISTMAS
(For All the Children)

Music by BARRY MANILOW
Lyric by BRUCE SUSSMAN and JACK FELDMAN

Moderately

To - night the stars shine ____ for the chil - dren
To - night be - longs to _____ all the chil - dren.

and light the way for dreams to fly.
To - night their joy rings through the air.

To - night our love comes wrapped in ____ rib - bons.
And so, we send our ten - der bless - ings

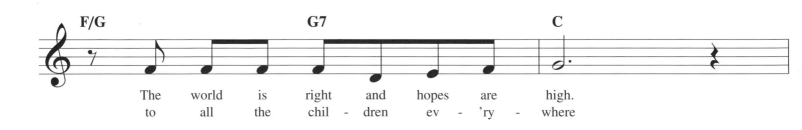

The world is right and hopes are high.
to all the chil - dren ev - 'ry - where

And from a dark and frost - ed win - dow a child ap -
to see the smiles and hear the laugh - ter; a time to

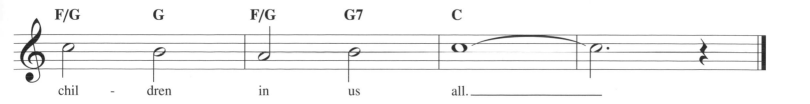

To Coda
E7
Am
pears to search the sky be - cause it's
give, a time to share be - cause it's
1
Dm
F/G
G
Christ - mas, be - cause it's Christ - mas.
2
A♭
C/G
Christ - mas for now and for - ev - er for all of the
Am
D
G7
C
chil - dren and for the chil - dren in us all.
G7
D.C. al Coda
(Verse 2)
CODA
A♭
Christ - mas for now and for -
C/G
Am
D
ev - er for all of the chil - dren and for the
F/G
G
F/G
G7
C
chil - dren in us all.

BLUE CHRISTMAS

Words and Music by BILLY HAYES
and JAY JOHNSON

With expression

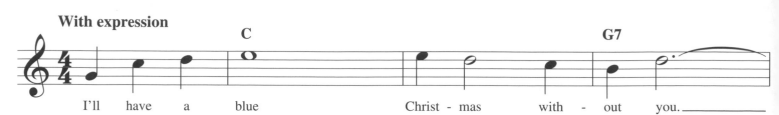

I'll have a blue Christ - mas with - out you. ___

___ I'll be so blue think - ing a - bout you. ___ Dec - o -

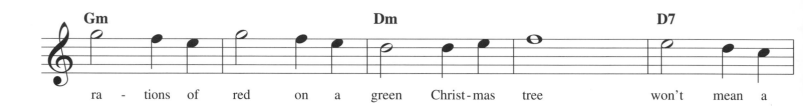

ra - tions of red on a green Christ - mas tree won't mean a

thing if you're not here with me. I'll have a blue Christ - mas, that's

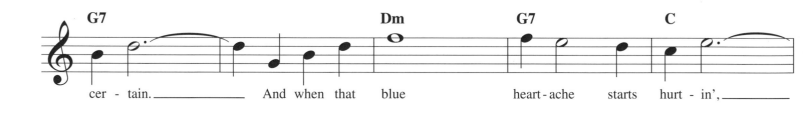

cer - tain. ___ And when that blue heart - ache starts hurt - in', ___

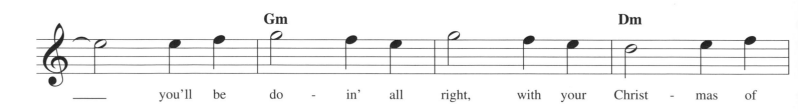

___ you'll be do - in' all right, with your Christ - mas of

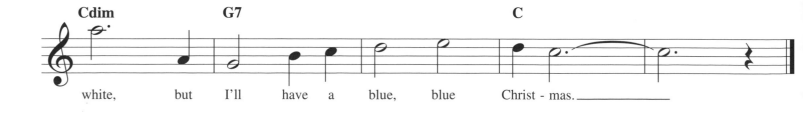

white, but I'll have a blue, blue Christ - mas. ___

BREATH OF HEAVEN
(Mary's Song)

Words and Music by AMY GRANT
and CHRIS EATON

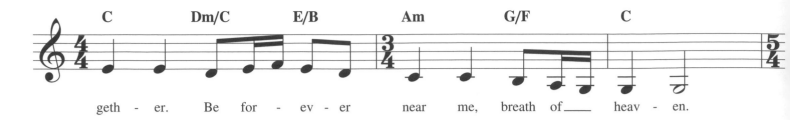

geth - er. Be for - ev - er near me, breath of_____ heav - en.

Breath of heav - en, light - en my dark - ness. Pour o - ver me Your

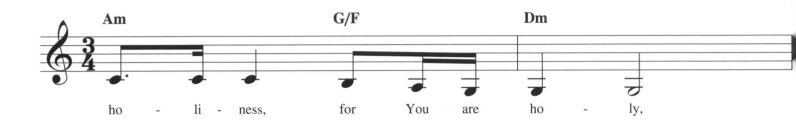

ho - li - ness, for You are ho - ly,

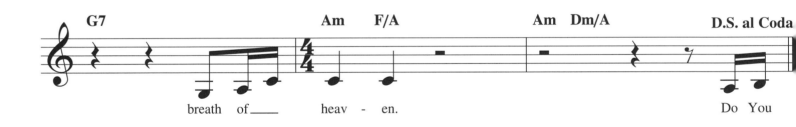

breath of_____ heav - en. Do You

CODA

plan._____ Help_____ me be strong,_____ help_____ me be,

_____ help_____ me. Breath of heav - en, hold me to-

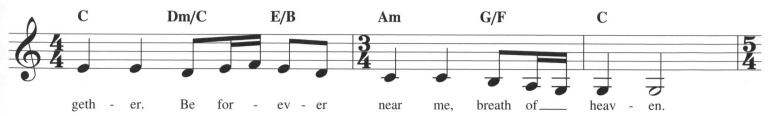

geth - er. Be for - ev - er near me, breath of____ heav - en.

Breath of heav - en, light - en my dark - ness. Pour o - ver me Your

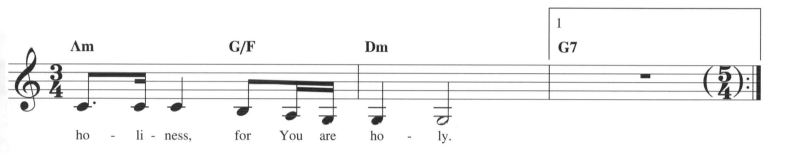

ho - li - ness, for You are ho - ly.

breath of____ heav - en, breath of____

heav - en, breath of____ heav - en.

BRAZILIAN SLEIGH BELLS

By PERCY FAITH

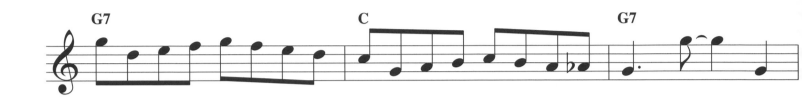

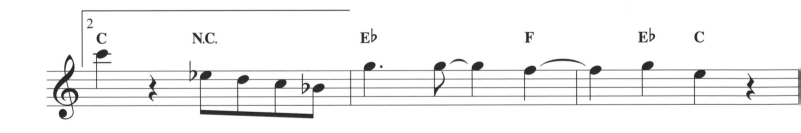

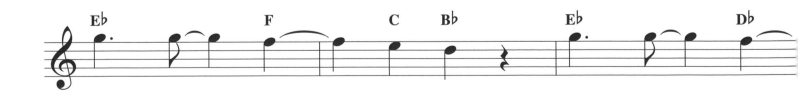

BRING A TORCH, JEANNETTE, ISABELLA

17th Century French Provençal Carol

Moderately

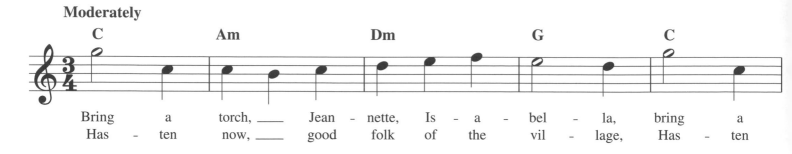

Bring a torch, ____ Jean - nette, Is - a - bel - la, bring a
Has - ten now, ____ good folk of the vil - lage, Has - ten

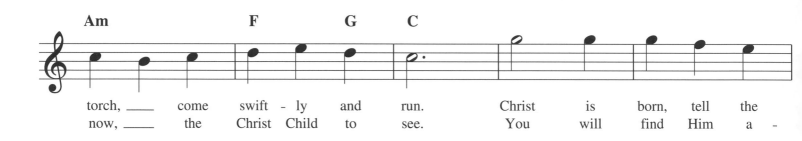

torch, ____ come swift - ly and run. Christ is born, tell the
now, ____ the Christ Child to see. You will find Him a -

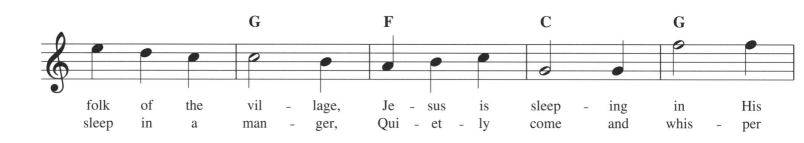

folk of the vil - lage, Je - sus is sleep - ing in His
sleep in a man - ger, Qui - et - ly come and whis - per

cra - dle, Ah, ah, Beau - ti - ful is the Moth - er,
soft - ly, Hush, hush, Peace - ful - ly now He slum - bers,

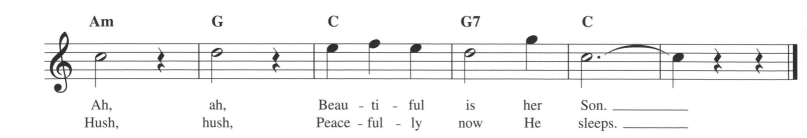

Ah, ah, Beau - ti - ful is her Son. _____
Hush, hush, Peace - ful - ly now He sleeps. _____

CAROLING, CAROLING

Words by WIHLA HUTSON
Music by ALFRED BURT

Joyfully

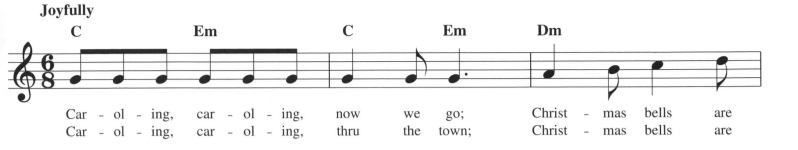

Car - ol - ing, car - ol - ing, now we go; Christ - mas bells are
Car - ol - ing, car - ol - ing, thru the town; Christ - mas bells are

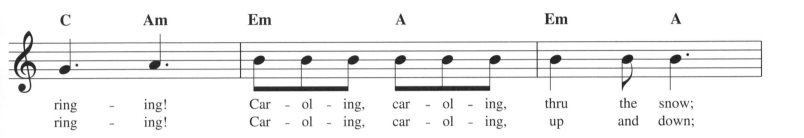

ring - ing! Car - ol - ing, car - ol - ing, thru the snow;
ring - ing! Car - ol - ing, car - ol - ing, up and down;

Christ - mas bells are ring - ing! Joy - ous voic - es
Christ - mas bells are ring - ing! Mark ye well the

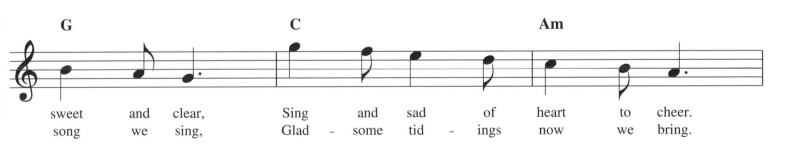

sweet and clear, Sing and sad of heart to cheer.
song we sing, Glad - some tid - ings now we bring.

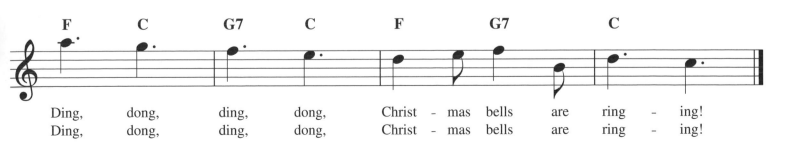

Ding, dong, ding, dong, Christ - mas bells are ring - ing!
Ding, dong, ding, dong, Christ - mas bells are ring - ing!

CHILD OF GOD

Words and Music by GRANT CUNNINGHAM
and MATT HUESMANN

With emotion

This is not ___ the way ___ I dreamed ___ the sto - ry would ___ un - fold: ___
I am just ___ a peas - ant girl ___ of sim - ple, hon - est means. ___

___ a sta - ble and ___ a bed ___
___ Who am I ___ to hold ___

___ of hay, ___ a night so clear ___ and cold. ___ The
___ the Sav - ior sent to set ___ men free, ___ to

on - ly Child ___ of God ___ be - got - ten, in my arms ___ I hold.
know the Child ___ that I ___ gave life ___ will give His life ___ for me? ___

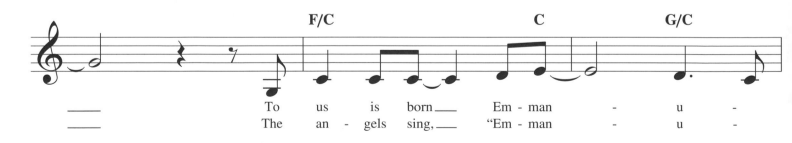

___ To us is born ___ Em - man - u -
The an - gels sing, ___ "Em - man - u -

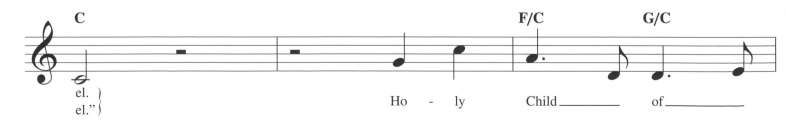

el. }
el." }   Ho - ly Child ___ of ___

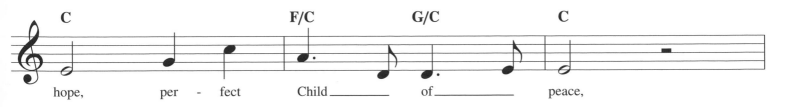

hope, per - fect Child _____ of _____ peace,

born to be _____ the Lord _____ of life _____ in _____ me. _____

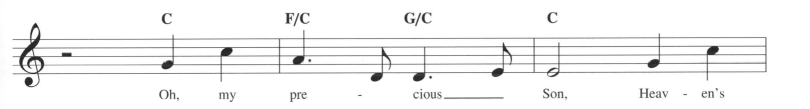

Oh, my pre - cious _____ Son, Heav - en's

Child _____ has _____ come to

make of me _____ a Child _____ of God.

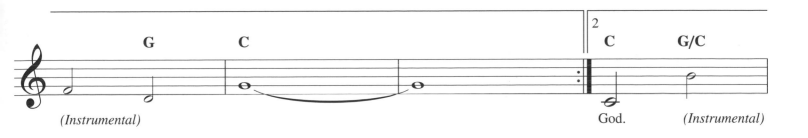

(Instrumental) God. *(Instrumental)*

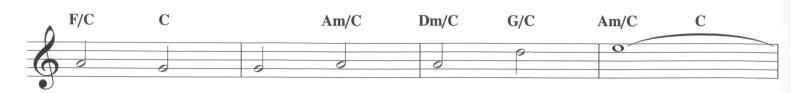

Oh, my

pre - cious Son, Heav - en's Child _____ has

come to make of me _____ a

child _____ of God. Oh, to

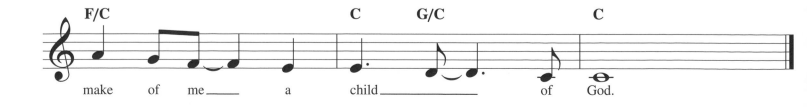

make of me _____ a child _____ of God.

THE CHIPMUNK SONG

Words and Music by
ROSS BAGDASARIAN

Moderately

Christ - mas,   Christ - mas   time   is   near,   Time   for

toys   and   time   for   cheer,   We've   been   good   but

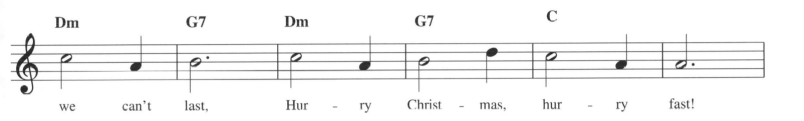

we   can't   last,   Hur - ry   Christ - mas,   hur - ry   fast!

Want   a   plane   that   loops   the   loop;   Me,   I

want   a   hu - la   hoop.   We   can   hard - ly

stand   the   wait.   Please   Christ - mas,   don't   be   late. ____

CHRISTMAS IS

Lyrics by SPENCE MAXWELL
Music by PERCY FAITH

Slowly

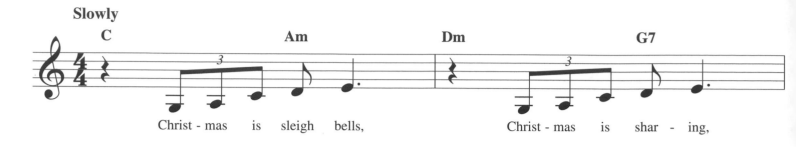

Christ - mas is sleigh bells,   Christ - mas is shar - ing,

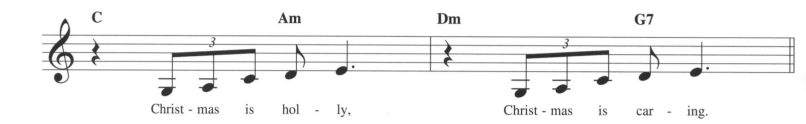

Christ - mas is hol - ly,   Christ - mas is car - ing.

Christ - mas is chil - dren who just can't___ go to sleep,
Christ - mas is car - ols to warm you___ in the snow,

Christ - mas is mem - 'ries the kind you___ al - ways keep,
Christ - mas is bed - time where no one___ wants to go,

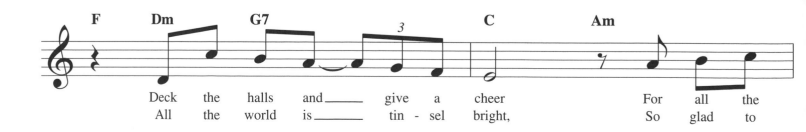

Deck the halls and___ give a cheer   For all the
All the world is___ tin - sel bright,   So glad to

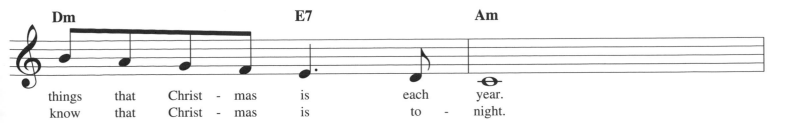

things   that   Christ - mas   is   each   year.
know   that   Christ - mas   is   to - night.

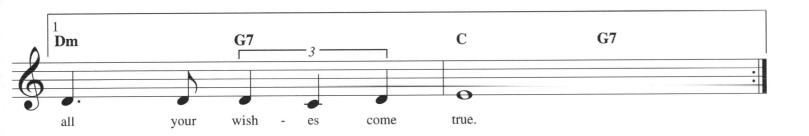

Christ - mas,_____   mer - ry   Christ - mas,_____   When
Christ - mas,_____   mer - ry   Christ - mas,_____   When

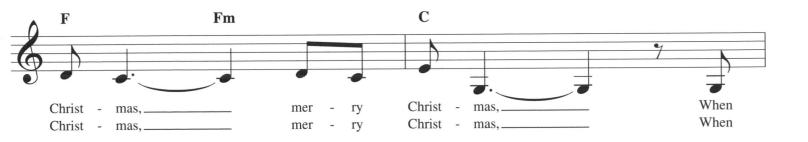

all   your   wish - es   come   true.

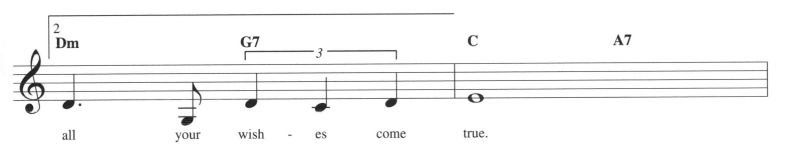

all   your   wish - es   come   true.

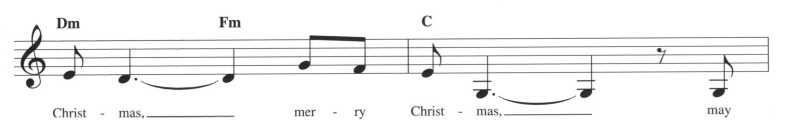

Christ - mas,_____   mer - ry   Christ - mas,_____   may

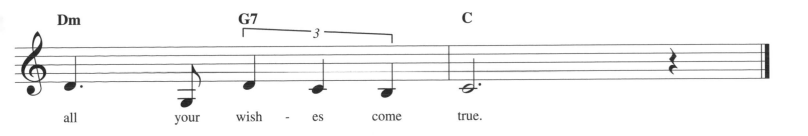

all   your   wish - es   come   true.

CHRISTMAS IS A-COMIN'
(May God Bless You)

Words and Music by
FRANK LUTHER

Moderately slow

When I'm feel - in' blue, an' when I'm feel - in' low,

then I start to think a - bout the hap - pi - est man I know. He

does - n't mind the snow an' he does - n't mind the rain, but

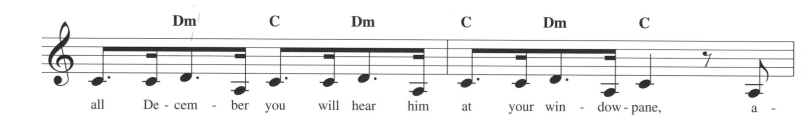

all De - cem - ber you will hear him at your win - dow - pane, a -

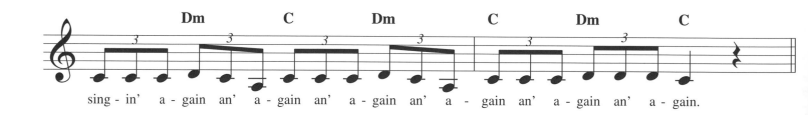

sing - in' a - gain an' a - gain an' a - gain an' a - gain an' a - gain an' a - gain.

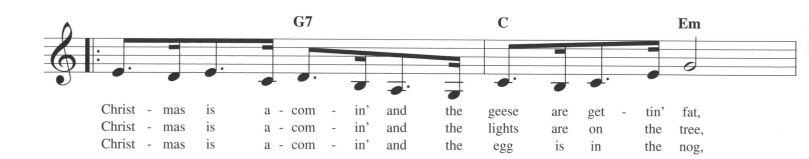

Christ - mas is a - com - in' and the geese are get - tin' fat,
Christ - mas is a - com - in' and the lights are on the tree,
Christ - mas is a - com - in' and the egg is in the nog,

THE CHRISTMAS SHOES

Words and Music by LEONARD AHLSTROM
and EDDIE CARSWELL

Moderately

Additional Verse

2. They counted pennies for what seemed like years,
   Then the cashier said, "Son, there's not enough here."
   He searched his pockets frantic'lly,
   Then he turned and he looked at me.
   He said, "Mama made Christmas good at our house,
   Though most years she just did without.
   Tell me, sir, what am I gonna do?
   Somehow I've gotta buy her these Christmas shoes."
   So, I laid the money down.
   I just had to help him out.
   And I'll never forget the look on his face when he said,
   "Mama's gonna look so great."
   Chorus

CHRISTMAS TIME IS HERE
from A CHARLIE BROWN CHRISTMAS

Words by LEE MENDELSON
Music by VINCE GUARALDI

THE CHRISTMAS SONG
(Chestnuts Roasting on an Open Fire)

Music and Lyric by MEL TORMÉ
and ROBERT WELLS

Slowly

Chest - nuts roast -ing on an o - pen fire, Jack Frost nip - ping at your

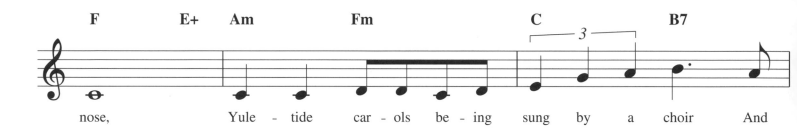

nose, Yule - tide car - ols be - ing sung by a choir And

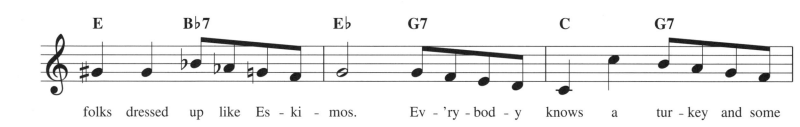

folks dressed up like Es - ki - mos. Ev - 'ry -bod - y knows a tur - key and some

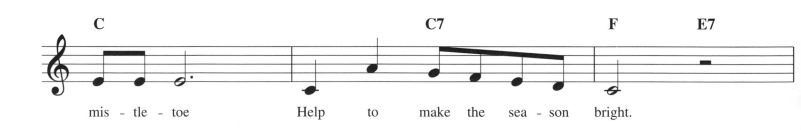

mis - tle - toe Help to make the sea - son bright.

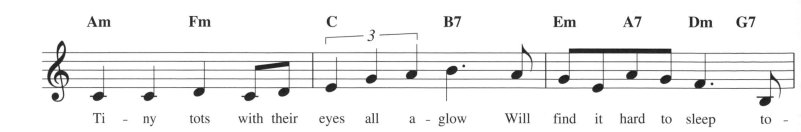

Ti - ny tots with their eyes all a - glow Will find it hard to sleep to -

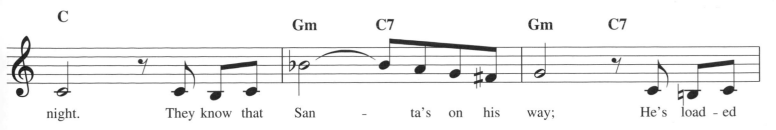

night. They know that San - ta's on his way; He's load - ed

lots of toys and good - ies on his sleigh And ev - 'ry

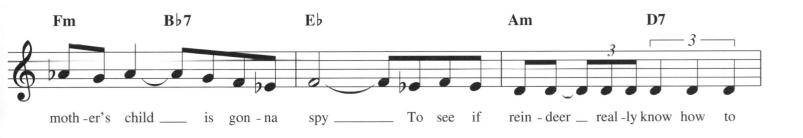

moth - er's child ___ is gon - na spy ___ To see if rein - deer ___ real - ly know how to

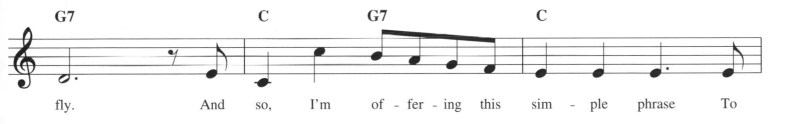

fly. And so, I'm of - fer - ing this sim - ple phrase To

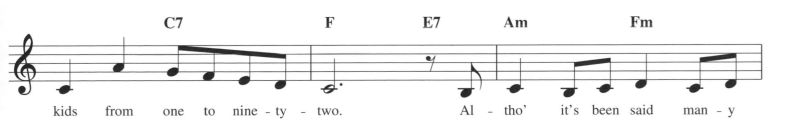

kids from one to nine - ty - two. Al - tho' it's been said man - y

times, man - y ways; "Mer - ry Christ - mas to you."

THE CHRISTMAS WALTZ

Words by SAMMY CAHN
Music by JULE STYNE

COVENTRY CAROL

Words by ROBERT CROO
Traditional English Melody

Tenderly

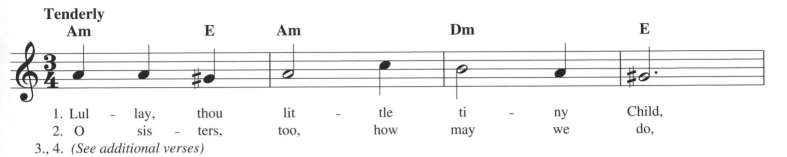

1. Lul - lay, thou lit - tle ti - ny Child,
2. O sis - ters, too, how may we do,

3., 4. *(See additional verses)*

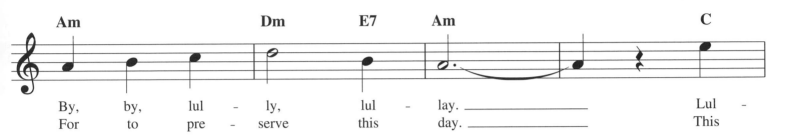

By, by, lul - ly, lul - lay. _____ Lul -
For to pre - serve this day. _____ This

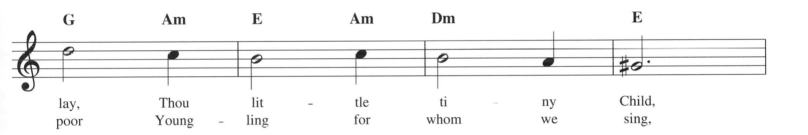

lay, Thou lit - tle ti - ny Child,
poor Young - ling for whom we sing,

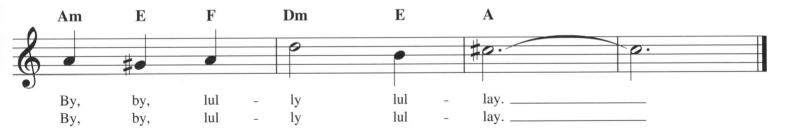

By, by, lul - ly lul - lay. _____
By, by, lul - ly lul - lay. _____

Additional Verses

3. Herod, the King
   In his raging,
   Charged he hath this day.
   His men of might,
   In his own sight,
   All young children to slay.

4. That woe is me,
   Poor child for thee!
   And ever morn and day,
   For thy parting
   Neither say nor sing
   By, by, lully, lullay.

CHRISTMASTIME

Words and Music by MICHAEL W. SMITH
and JOANNA CARLSON

DECK THE HALL

Traditional Welsh Carol

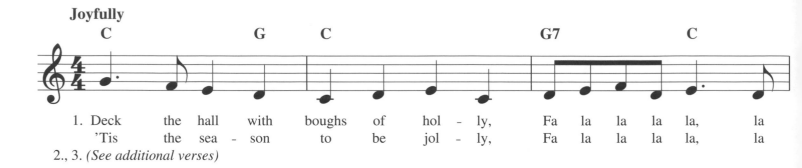

1. Deck the hall with boughs of hol - ly, Fa la la la la, la
'Tis the sea - son to be jol - ly, Fa la la la la, la

2., 3. *(See additional verses)*

la la la.
la la la. Don we now our gay ap - par - rel,

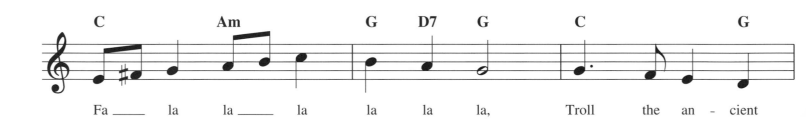

Fa ___ la la ___ la la la la, Troll the an - cient

Yule - tide car - ol, Fa la la la la, la la la la.

Additional Verses

2. See the blazing Yule before us, Fa la la la la la, la la la la.
   Strike the harp and join the chorus, Fa la la la la la, la la la la.
   Follow me in merry measure, Fa la la la la la la la,
   While I tell of Yuletide treasure, Fa la la la la la, la la la la.

3. Fast away the old year passes, Fa la la la la la, la la la la.
   Hail the new, ye lads and lasses, Fa la la la la la, la la la la.
   Sing we joyous all together, Fa la la la la la la la,
   Heedless of the wind and weather, Fa la la la la la, la la la la.

DING DONG! MERRILY ON HIGH!

French Carol

With spirit

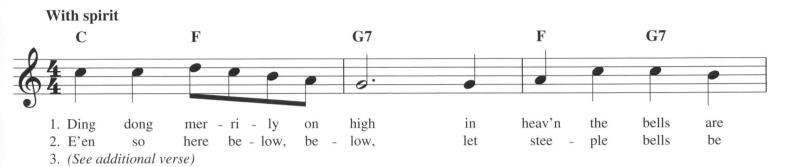

1. Ding   dong   mer - ri - ly   on   high   in   heav'n   the   bells   are
2. E'en   so   here   be - low,   be - low,   let   stee - ple   bells   be
3. *(See additional verse)*

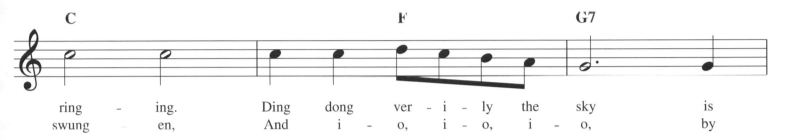

ring   -   ing.   Ding   dong   ver - i - ly   the   sky   is
swung   -   en,   And   i   -   o,   i   -   o,   i   -   o,   by

Chorus

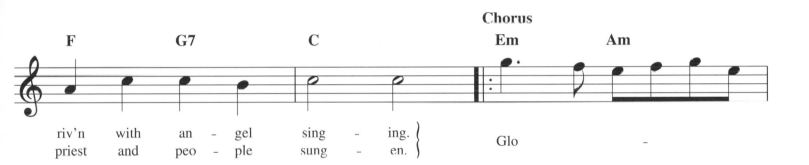

riv'n   with   an - gel   sing   -   ing.   }   Glo   -
priest   and   peo - ple   sung   -   en.   }

-   ri - a,   Ho - san - na   in   ex - cel - sis!

Additional Verse

3. Pray you, dutifully prime your matin chime, ye ringers;
   May you beautifully rime your evetime song, ye singers.
   Chorus

DO THEY KNOW IT'S CHRISTMAS?

Words and Music by M. URE
and B. GELDOF

It's Christ - mas - time, there's no need to be a - fraid. __

At Christ - mas - time, we let in light __ and we ban-ish shade. ____

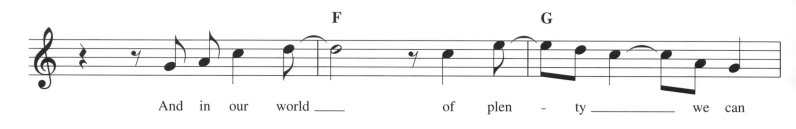

And in our world ____ of plen - ty _____ we can

spread a smile __ of joy _____ Throw your arms ___ a - round __ the world __

____ at Christ - mas - time. ___ But say a prayer,

to pray for the oth - er ones _____ at Christ - mas - time. It's

hard, but __ when you're hav - ing fun _____ there's __ a __ world out - side your win -

FELIZ NAVIDAD

Music and Lyrics by
JOSÉ FELICIANO

Fe - liz Na - vi - dad. _____ Fe - liz Na - vi - dad. _____ Fe - liz Na - vi -

dad. Pros - pe - ro a - ño y fe - li - ci - dad. _____ Fe - liz Na - vi -

I want to wish you a _____

Mer - ry Christ - mas, with lots of pres - ents to make you hap - py. I want to wish you a

Mer - ry Christ - mas from the bot - tom of my heart. _____ I want to wish you a

Mer - ry Christ - mas, with mis - tle - toe and __ lots of cheer, __ with lots of laugh - ter through -

out the years from the bot - tom of my heart. _____ Fe - liz Na - vi -

DO YOU HEAR WHAT I HEAR

Words and Music by NOEL REGNEY
and GLORIA SHAYNE

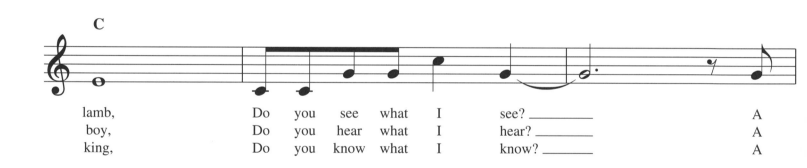

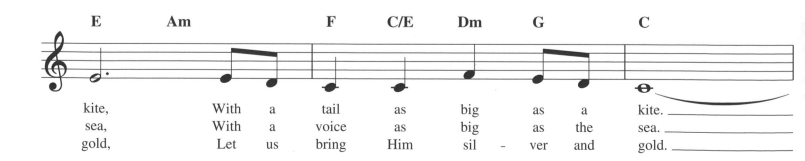

1, 2 **3** **Bb**

Said the _____ Said the king to the peo - ple ev - 'ry -
Said the

C

where, Lis - ten to what I say! _____

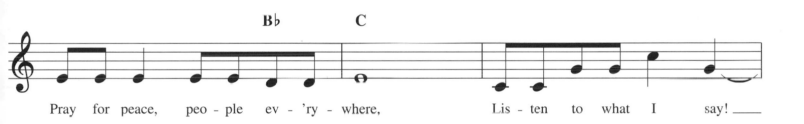

Bb **C**

Pray for peace, peo - ple ev - 'ry - where, Lis - ten to what I say! _____

Am **Em**

_____ The Child, the Child, sleep - ing in the night. He will

F **G** **F** **E** **Am** **F** **C/E**

bring us good - ness and light, He will bring us

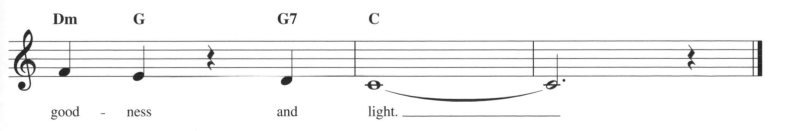

Dm **G** **G7** **C**

good - ness and light. _____

EMMANUEL

Words and Music by
MICHAEL W. SMITH

Moderately

Em - man - u - el, Em - man - u - el.

Won - der - ful Coun - sel - or, _____ Lord of life, Lord of all. ____

_____ He's _ the Prince of Peace, Might - y God, Ho - ly One, _____ Em -

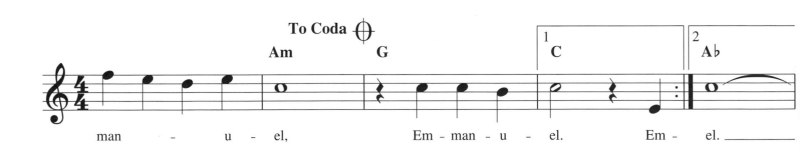

man - u - el, Em - man - u - el. Em - el. _____

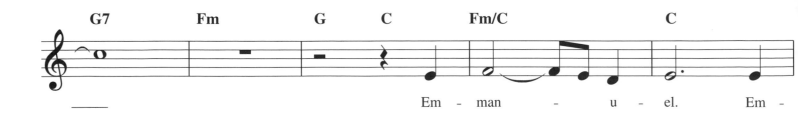

_____ Em - man - u - el. Em -

THE FIRST NOËL

17th Century English Carol
Music from W. Sandys' *Christmas Carols*

THE FRIENDLY BEASTS

Traditional English Carol

Tenderly

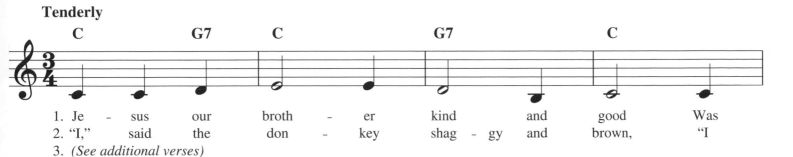

1. Je - sus our broth - er kind and good Was
2. "I," said the don - key shag - gy and brown, "I
3. *(See additional verses)*

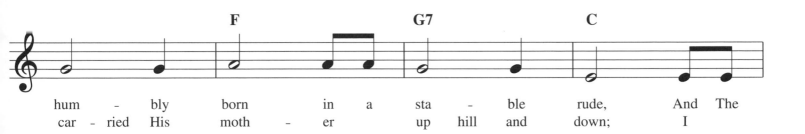

hum - bly born in a sta - ble rude, And The
car - ried His moth - er up hill and down; I

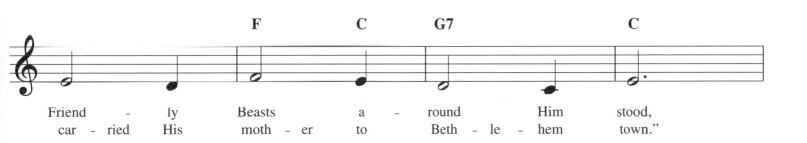

Friend - ly Beasts a - round Him stood,
car - ried His moth - er to Beth - le - hem town."

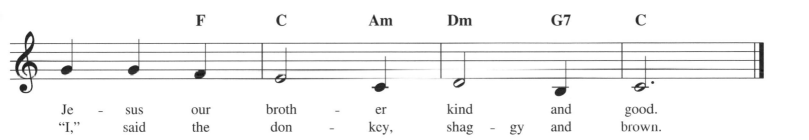

Je - sus our broth - er kind and good.
"I," said the don - key, shag - gy and brown.

Additional Verses

3. "I," said the cow all white and red,
   "I gave Him my manger for His bed;
   I gave Him my hay to pillow His head."
   "I," said the cow all white and red.

4. "I," said the sheep with the curly horn,
   "I gave Him my wool for His blanket warm;
   He wore my coat on Christmas morn."
   "I," said the sheep with the curly horn.

5. "I," said the dove from the rafters high,
   "I cooed Him to sleep that He would not cry;
   We cooed Him to sleep, my mate and I."
   "I," said the dove from the rafters high.

6. Thus every beast by some good spell,
   In the stable dark was glad to tell
   Of the gift he gave Emmanuel,
   The gift he gave Emmanuel.

FROSTY THE SNOW MAN

Words and Music by STEVE NELSON
and JACK ROLLINS

Moderately

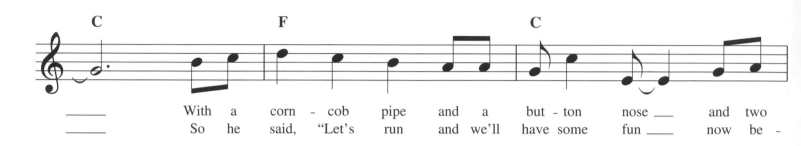

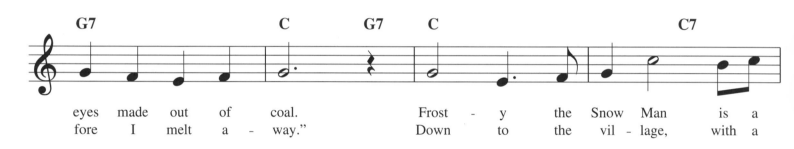

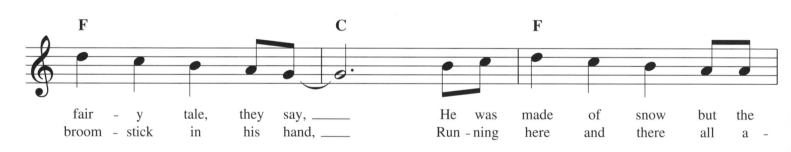

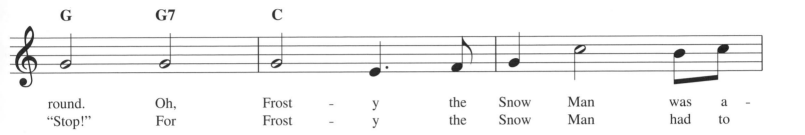

when they placed it on his head he be - gan to dance a -
on - ly paused a mo - ment when ____ he heard him hol - ler,

round. Oh, Frost - y the Snow Man was a -
"Stop!" For Frost - y the Snow Man had to

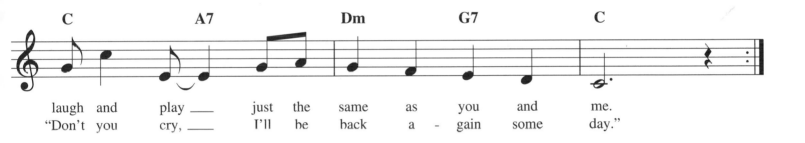

live as he could be, ____ And the chil - dren say he could
hur - ry on his way, ____ But he waved good - bye say - in'

laugh and play ____ just the same as you and me.
"Don't you cry, ____ I'll be back a - gain some day."

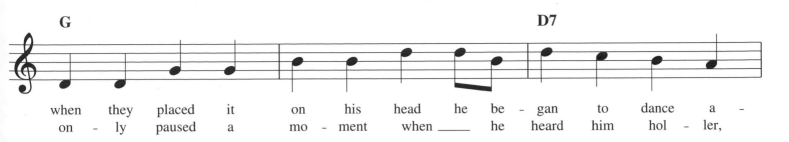

Thump - et - y thump thump, thump - et - y thump thump. Look at Frost - y go.

Thump - et - y thump thump, thump - et - y thump thump. O - ver the hills of snow.

GO, TELL IT ON THE MOUNTAIN

African-American Spiritual
Verses by JOHN W. WORK, JR.

Moderately

Go, tell it on the moun - tain, O - ver the hills and ev - 'ry - where;

Last time Fine

Go, tell it on the moun - tain That Je - sus Christ _ is born.

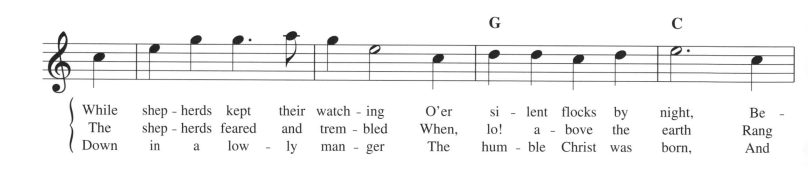

While shep - herds kept their watch - ing O'er si - lent flocks by night, Be -
The shep - herds feared and trem - bled When, lo! a - bove the earth Rang
Down in a low - ly man - ger The hum - ble Christ was born, And

hold, through - out the heav - ens There shone a ho - ly light. _____
out the an - gel cho - rus That hailed our Sav - ior's birth. _____
God sent us sal - va - tion That bless - ed Christ - mas morn. _____

GOD REST YE MERRY, GENTLEMEN

19th Century English Carol

Moderately

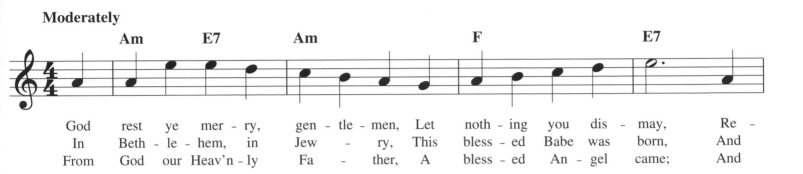

God rest ye mer - ry, gen - tle - men, Let noth - ing you dis - may, Re -
In Beth - le - hem, in Jew - ry, This bless - ed Babe was born, And
From God our Heav'n - ly Fa - ther, A bless - ed An - gel came; And

mem - ber Christ our Sav - iour Was born on Christ - mas Day, To
laid with - in a man - ger, Up - on this bless - ed morn; That
un - to cer - tain Shep - herds, Brought tid - ings of the same; How

save us all from Sa - tan's pow'r, When we were gone a -
which His Moth - er Mar - y, Did noth - ing take in
that in Beth - le - hem was born The Son of God by

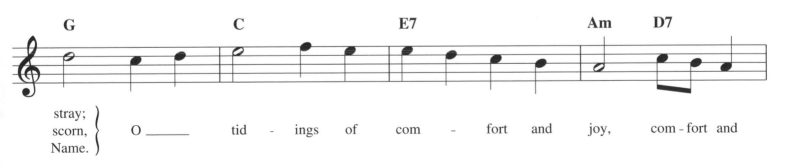

stray;
scorn,   O _____ tid - ings of com - fort and joy, com - fort and
Name.

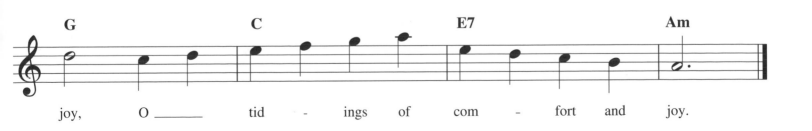

joy, O _____ tid - ings of com - fort and joy.

GOOD CHRISTIAN MEN, REJOICE

14th Century Latin Text
Translated by JOHN MASON NEALE
14th Century German Melody

With spirit

Good Chris - tian men, re - joice, _____ With heart and soul and
Good Chris - tian men, re - joice, _____ With heart and soul and
Good Chris - tian men, re - joice, _____ With heart and soul and

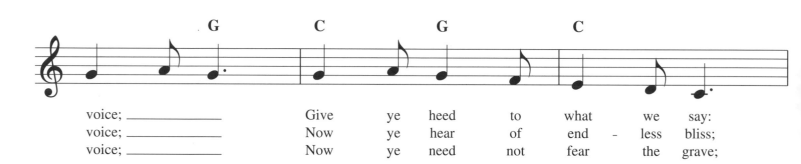

voice; _____ Give ye heed to what we say:
voice; _____ Now ye hear of end - less bliss;
voice; _____ Now ye need not fear the grave;

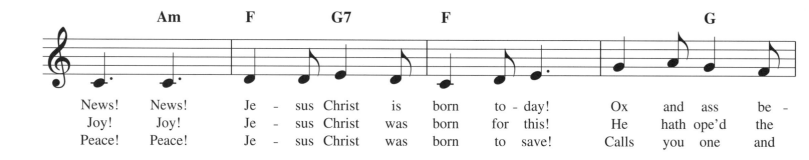

News! News! Je - sus Christ is born to - day! Ox and ass be -
Joy! Joy! Je - sus Christ was born for this! He hath ope'd the
Peace! Peace! Je - sus Christ was born to save! Calls you one and

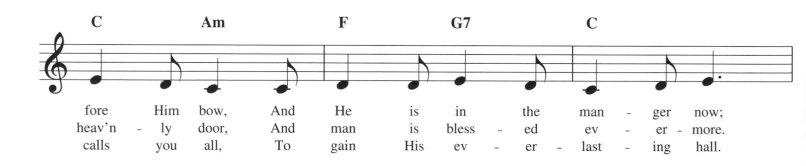

fore Him bow, And He is in the man - ger now;
heav'n - ly door, And man is bless - ed ev - er - more.
calls you all, To gain His ev - er - last - ing hall.

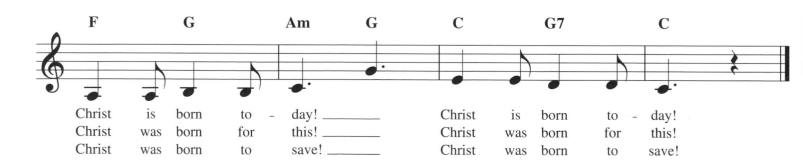

Christ is born to - day! _____ Christ is born to - day!
Christ was born for this! _____ Christ was born for this!
Christ was born to save! _____ Christ was born to save!

GOOD KING WENCESLAS

Words by JOHN M. NEALE
Music from *Piae Cantiones*

Moderately

1. Good King Wen - ces - las looked out   On the feast of Ste - phen,
2. "Hith - er, page, and stand by me,   If thou know'st it, tell - ing,
3.-5. *(See additional verses)*

When the snow lay 'round a - bout,   Deep, and crisp, and e - ven;
Yon - der pea - sant, who is he?   Where and what his dwell - ing?"

Bright - ly shone the moon that night,   Though the frost was cru - el,
"Sire, he lives a good league hence,   Un - der - neath the moun - tain,

When a poor man came in sight,   Gath - 'ring win - ter fu - el.
Right a - gainst the for - est fence,   By Saint Ag - nes' foun - tain."

Additional Verses

3. "Bring me flesh, and bring me wine,
Bring me pine-logs hither:
Thou and I will see him dine,
When we bear them thither."
Page and monarch, forth they went,
Forth they went together;
Through the rude wind's wild lament
And the bitter weather.

4. "Sire, the night is darker now,
And the wind blows stronger;
Fails my heart, I know not how;
I can go no longer."
"Mark my footsteps, good my page;
Tread thou in them boldly:
Thou shalt find the winter's rage
Freeze thy blood less coldly."

5. In his master's steps he trod,
Where the snow lay dinted;
Heat was in the very sod
Which the saint had printed.
Therefore, Christian men, be sure,
Wealth or rank possessing,
Ye who now will bless the poor,
Shall yourselves find blessing.

GRANDMA GOT RUN OVER BY A REINDEER

Words and Music by
RANDY BROOKS

Moderately bright

Grand-ma got run o-ver by a rein-deer   walk-ing home from our house Christ-mas

Eve.   You can say there's no such thing as San-ta,   but

as for me and Grand-pa, we be-lieve.   1. She'd been drink-ing too much
2., 3. (*See additional lyrics*)

egg-nog   and we begged her not to go,

but she for-got her med-i-ca-tion,   and she stag-gered out the door in-to the

snow.   When we found her Christ-mas morn-ing

G7   **C**   **C7**

at the scene of the at - tack,   she had hoof-prints on her

1st and 2nd time D.C.
3rd time D.C. al Coda

F   **G**   **C**

fore - head,   and in - crim - i - nat - ing Claus marks on her back.

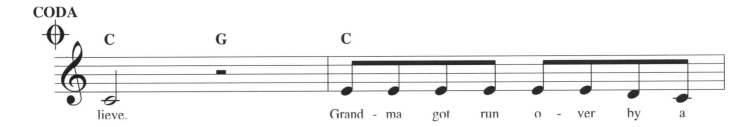

CODA

C   **G**   **C**

lieve.   Grand - ma got run o - ver by a

F

rein - deer   walk - ing home from our house Christ - mas Eve.

C   **G**

You can say there's no such thing as San - ta,   but as for me and Grand - pa, we be -

C   **G**   **C**

lieve._____

Additional Lyrics

2. Now we're all so proud of Grandpa,
   He's been taking this so well.
   See him in there watching football,
   Drinking beer and playing cards with Cousin Mel.
   It's not Christmas without Grandma.
   All the family's dressed in black,
   And we just can't help but wonder;
   Should we open up her gifts or send them back?
   Chorus

3. Now the goose is on the table,
   And the pudding made of fig,
   And the blue and silver candles,
   That would just have matched the hair in Grandma's wig.
   I've warned all my friends and neighbors,
   Better watch out for yourselves.
   They should never give a license
   To a man who drives a sleigh and plays with elves.
   Chorus

HAPPY HOLIDAY
from the Motion Picture Irving Berlin's HOLIDAY INN

Words and Music by
IRVING BERLIN

HARK! THE HERALD ANGELS SING

Words by CHARLES WESLEY
Altered by GEORGE WHITEFIELD
Music by FELIX MENDELSSOHN-BARTHOLDY
Arranged by WILLIAM H. CUMMINGS

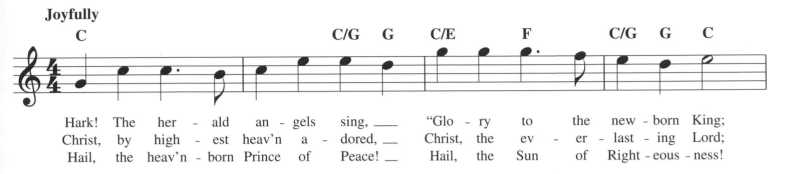

Hark! The her - ald an - gels sing, ___ "Glo - ry to the new - born King;
Christ, by high - est heav'n a - dored, ___ Christ, the ev - er - last - ing Lord;
Hail, the heav'n - born Prince of Peace! ___ Hail, the Sun of Right - eous - ness!

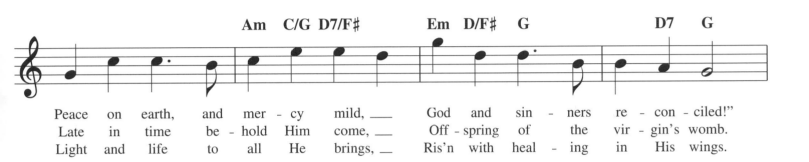

Peace on earth, and mer - cy mild, ___ God and sin - ners re - con - ciled!"
Late in time be - hold Him come, ___ Off - spring of the vir - gin's womb.
Light and life to all He brings, ___ Ris'n with heal - ing in His wings.

Joy - ful all ye na - tions, rise, ___ Join the tri - umph of the skies; ___
Veil'd in flesh the God - head see: ___ Hail th'in - car - nate De - i - ty, ___
Mild He lays His glo - ry by, ___ Born that man no more may die, ___

With th'an - gel - ic host pro - claim, "Christ is ___ born in Beth - le - hem!"
Pleased as Man with men to dwell, Je - sus ___ our Em - man - u - el!
Born to raise the sons of earth, Born to ___ give them sec - ond birth.

Hark! The her - ald an - gels sing, "Glo - ry ___ to the new - born King!"

HAPPY XMAS
(War Is Over)

Words and Music by JOHN LENNON
and YOKO ONO

HARD CANDY CHRISTMAS
from THE BEST LITTLE WHOREHOUSE IN TEXAS

Words and Music by
CAROL HALL

HERE COMES SANTA CLAUS
(Right Down Santa Claus Lane)

Words and Music by GENE AUTRY
and OAKLEY HALDEMAN

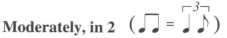

Moderately, in 2

Here comes San - ta Claus! Here comes San - ta Claus! Right down San - ta Claus   Lane!

Vix - en and Blitz - en and all his rein - deer are pull - ing on the
He's got a bag that is filled with toys for the boys and girls a -
He does - n't care if you're rich or poor, for he loves you just the
He'll come a - round when the chimes ring out; then it's Christ - mas morn a -

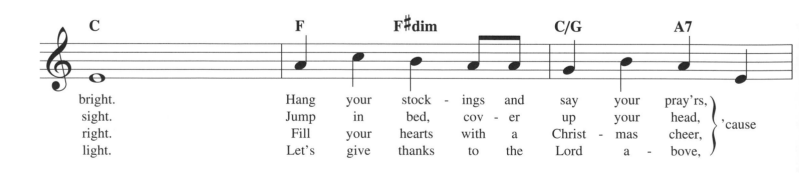

rein. Bells are ring - ing, chil - dren sing - ing, all is mer - ry and
gain. Hear those sleigh bells jin - gle jan - gle, what a beau - ti - ful
same. San - ta knows that we're God's chil - dren; that makes ev - 'ry - thing
gain. Peace on earth will come to all if we just fol - low the

bright. Hang your stock - ings and say your pray'rs,
sight. Jump in bed, cov - er up your head,
right. Fill your hearts with a Christ - mas cheer,
light. Let's give thanks to the Lord a - bove,   'cause

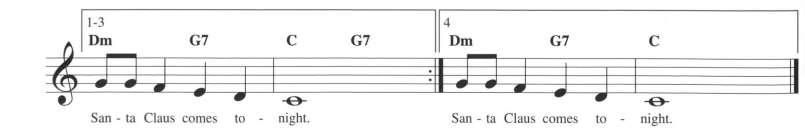

San - ta Claus comes to - night.   San - ta Claus comes to - night.

THE HOLLY AND THE IVY

18th Century English Carol

Additional Verses

4. The holly bears a prickle,
   As sharp as any thorn,
   And Mary bore sweet Jesus Christ,
   On Christmas Day in the morn.
   Refrain

5. The holly bears a bark,
   As bitter as any gall,
   And Mary bore sweet Jesus Christ,
   For to redeem us all.
   Refrain

A HOLLY JOLLY CHRISTMAS

Music and Lyrics by
JOHNNY MARKS

I HEARD THE BELLS ON CHRISTMAS DAY

Words by HENRY WADSWORTH LONGFELLOW
Music by JOHN BAPTISTE CALKIN

Slowly

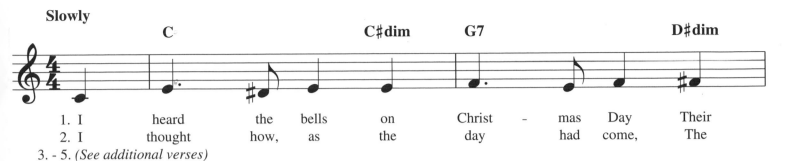

1. I heard the bells on Christ - mas Day Their
2. I thought how, as the day had come, The

3. - 5. *(See additional verses)*

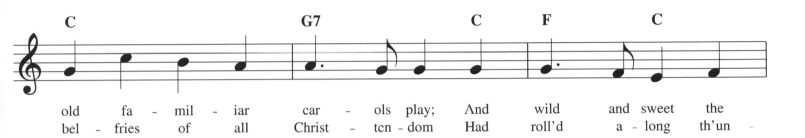

old fa - mil - iar car - ols play; And wild and sweet the
bel - fries of all Christ - ten - dom Had roll'd a - long th'un -

words re - peat Of peace on earth, good will to men.
bro - ken song Of peace on earth, good will to men.

Additional Verses

3. And in despair I bow'd my head:
   "There is no peace on earth," I said,
   "For hate is strong, and mocks the song
   Of peace on earth, good will to men."

4. Then pealed the bells more loud and deep:
   "God is not dead, nor doth He sleep;
   The wrong shall fail, the right prevail,
   With peace on earth good will to men."

5. Till, ringing, singing on its way,
   The world revolved from night to day,
   A voice, a chime, a chant sublime,
   Of peace on earth, good will to men!

(There's No Place Like)
HOME FOR THE HOLIDAYS

Words by AL STILLMAN
Music by ROBERT ALLEN

Moderately

Oh, there's no place like home for the hol - i - days; _____ 'Cause no

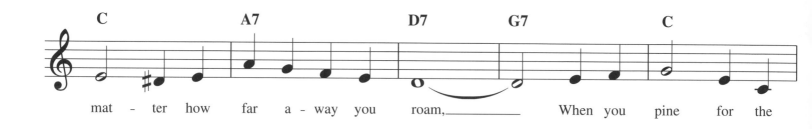

mat - ter how far a - way you roam, _____ When you pine for the

sun - shine of a friend - ly gaze, _____ for the hol - i - days you

can't beat home sweet home. I met a man who lives in Ten - nes - see and

he was head - in' for Penn - syl - va - nia and some home - made pump - kin

pie. From Penn - syl - va - nia folks are trav - 'lin' down to Dix - ie's sun - ny

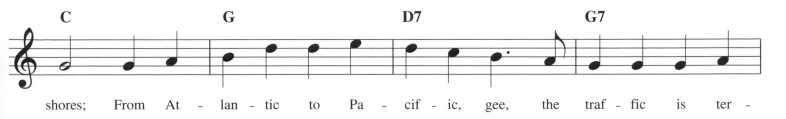

shores; From At - lan - tic to Pa - cif - ic, gee, the traf - fic is ter -

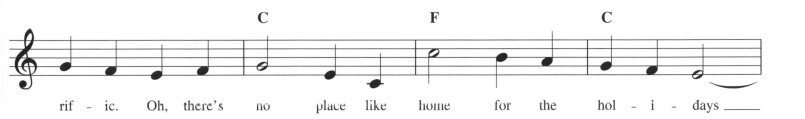

rif - ic. Oh, there's no place like home for the hol - i - days _____

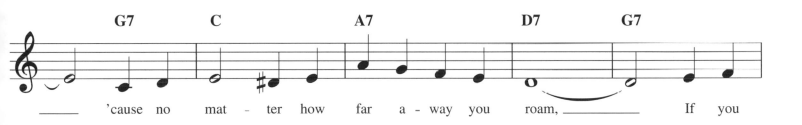

_____ 'cause no mat - ter how far a - way you roam, _____ If you

want to be hap - py in a mil - lion ways _____ For the

hol - i - days you can't beat home, sweet home. _____ Oh, there's

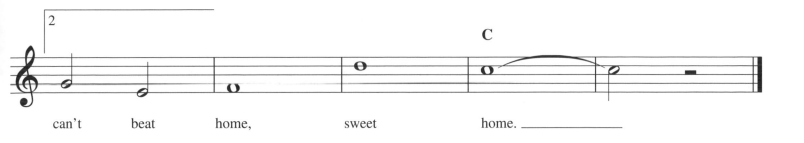

can't beat home, sweet home. _____

I HEARD THE BELLS ON CHRISTMAS DAY

Words by HENRY WADSWORTH LONGFELLOW
Adapted by JOHNNY MARKS
Music by JOHNNY MARKS

I heard the bells on Christ - mas day, their old fa - mil - iar
in de - spair, I bowed my head, "There is no peace on

car - ols play: And wild and sweet the words re - peat, of
earth," I said, "For hate is strong and mocks the song of

peace on earth, good will to men. I thought, as now this
peace on earth, good will to men." Then pealed the bells more

day had come, the bel - fries of all Chris - ten - dom had
loud and deep, "God is not dead, nor doth He sleep, the

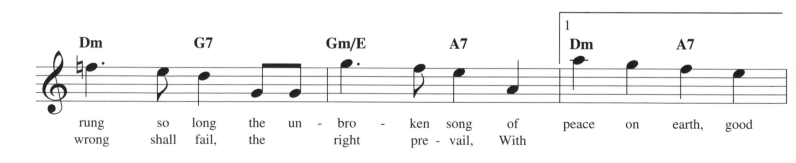

rung so long the un - bro - ken song of peace on earth, good
wrong shall fail, the right pre - vail, With

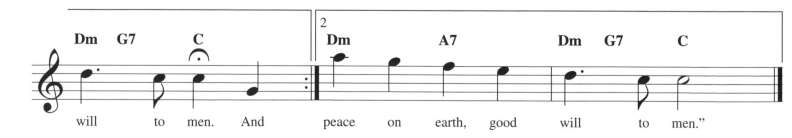

will to men. And peace on earth, good will to men."

I SAW MOMMY KISSING SANTA CLAUS

Words and Music by
TOMMIE CONNOR

I WISH EVERYDAY COULD BE LIKE CHRISTMAS

Words and Music by DAVID ERWIN
and JIM CARTER

I WONDER AS I WANDER

By JOHN JACOB NILES

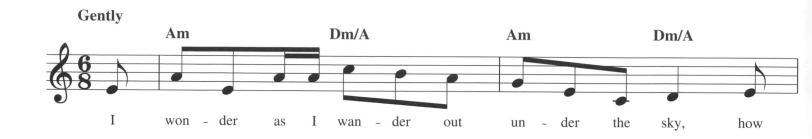

I won – der as I wan – der out un – der the sky, how

Je – sus the Sav – ior did come for to die for poor on – 'ry peo – ple like

you and like I... I won – der as I wan – der out un – der the sky. When

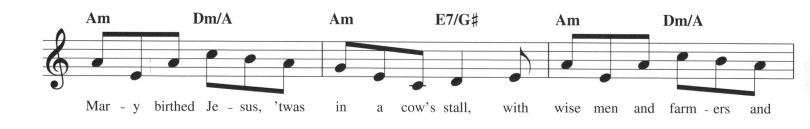

Mar – y birthed Je – sus, 'twas in a cow's stall, with wise men and farm – ers and

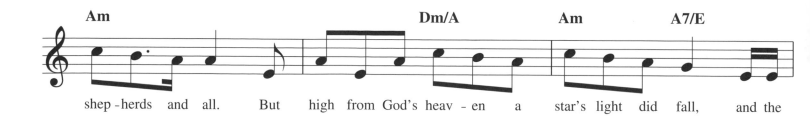

shep – herds and all. But high from God's heav – en a star's light did fall, and the

79

prom - ise of ag - es it then did re - call. If Je - sus had want - ed for

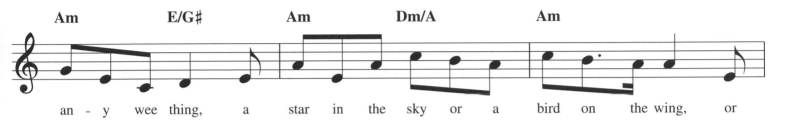

an - y wee thing, a star in the sky or a bird on the wing, or

all of God's an - gels in heav'n for to sing, He sure - ly could have it, 'cause

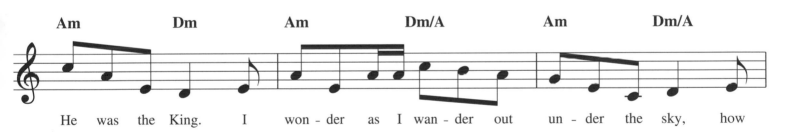

He was the King. I won - der as I wan - der out un - der the sky, how

Je - sus the Sav - ior did come for to die for poor on - 'ry peo - ple like

you and like I... I won - der as I wan - der out un - der the sky.

I'LL BE HOME FOR CHRISTMAS

Words and Music by KIM GANNON
and WALTER KENT

Moderately

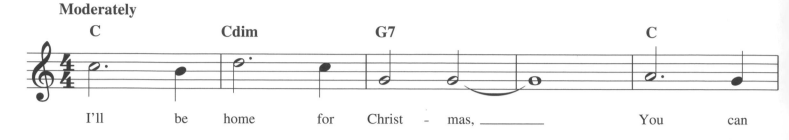

I'll be home for Christ - mas, _____ You can

plan on me. _____ Please have snow and

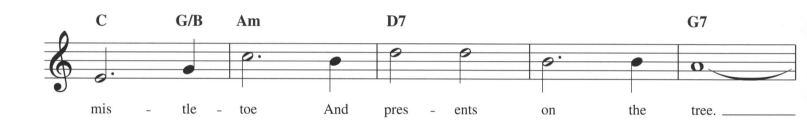

mis - tle - toe And pres - ents on the tree. _____

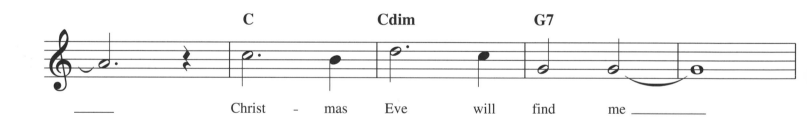

_____ Christ - mas Eve will find me _____

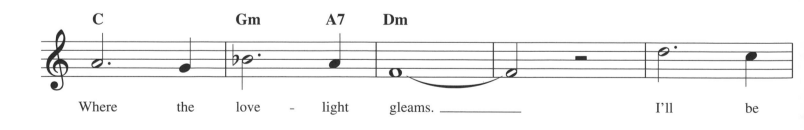

Where the love - light gleams. _____ I'll be

home for Christ - mas, If on - ly in my dreams. _____

IN THE BLEAK MIDWINTER

Poem by CHRISTINA ROSSETTI
Music by GUSTAV HOLST

Moderately

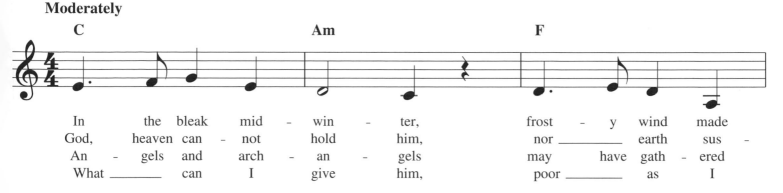

In the bleak mid - win - ter, frost - y wind made
God, heaven can - not hold him, nor ___ earth sus -
An - gels and arch - an - gels may have gath - ered
What ___ can I give him, poor ___ as I

moan, earth stood hard as i - ron,
tain; heaven and earth shall flee a - way
there, cher - u - bim and ser - a - phim
am? If I were a shep - herd,

wa - ter like a stone; snow had fall - en, snow on snow,
when he comes to reign. In the bleak mid - win - ter a
throng - ed the air; but his moth - er on - ly,
I would bring a lamb; if I were a Wise Man,

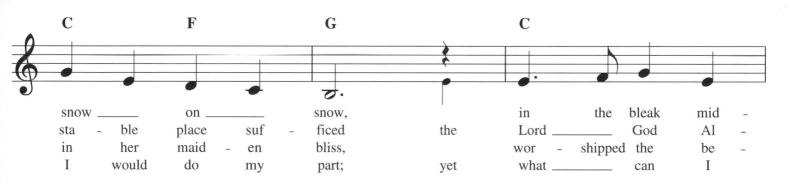

snow ___ on ___ snow, in the bleak mid -
sta - ble place suf - ficed the Lord ___ God Al -
in her maid - en bliss, wor - shipped the be -
I would do my part; yet what ___ can I

1-3 | 4

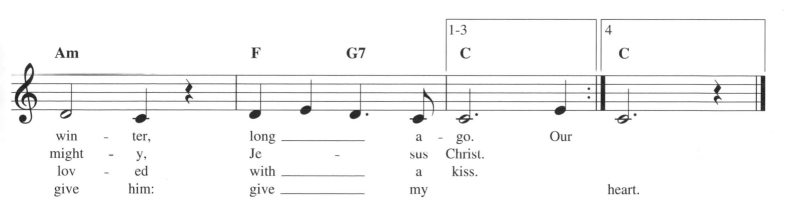

win - ter, long ___ a - go. Our
might - y, Je - sus Christ.
lov - ed with ___ a kiss.
give him: give ___ my heart.

I'VE GOT MY LOVE TO KEEP ME WARM
from the 20th Century Fox Motion Picture ON THE AVENUE

Words and Music by
IRVING BERLIN

Bright jump tempo

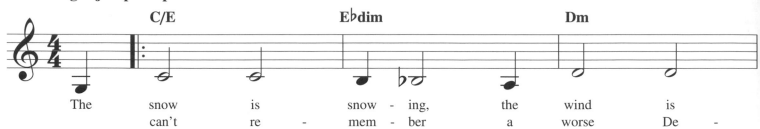

The snow is snow - ing, the wind is
can't re - mem - ber a worse De -

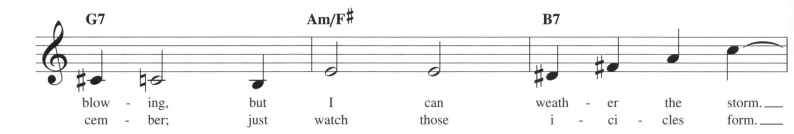

blow - ing, but I can weath - er the storm.
cem - ber; just watch those i - ci - cles form.

What do I care how
What do I care if

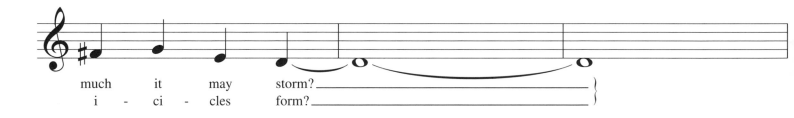

much it may storm?
i - ci - cles form?

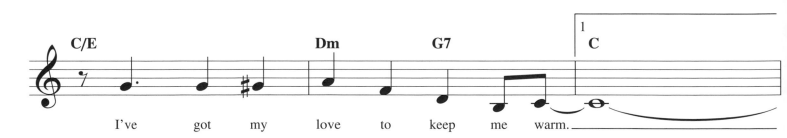

I've got my love to keep me warm.

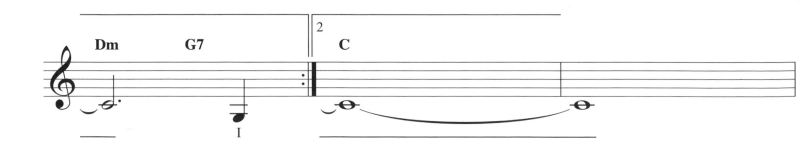

IT CAME UPON THE MIDNIGHT CLEAR

Words by EDMUND HAMILTON SEARS
Music by RICHARD STORRS WILLIS

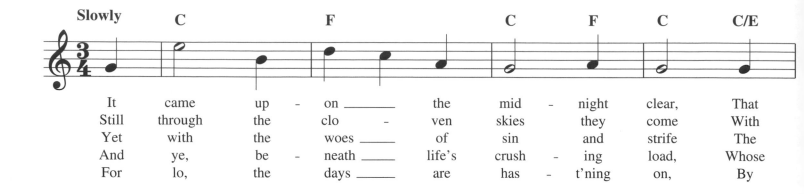

It came up - on _____ the mid - night clear, That
Still through the clo - ven skies they come With
Yet with the woes _____ of sin and strife The
And ye, be - neath _____ life's crush - ing load, Whose
For lo, the days _____ are has - t'ning on, By

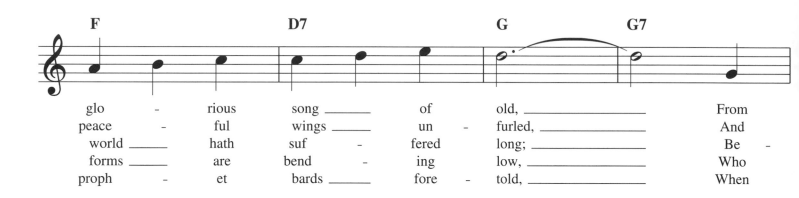

glo - rious song _____ of old, _____ From
peace - ful wings _____ un - furled, _____ And
world _____ hath suf - fered long; _____ Be -
forms _____ are bend - ing low, _____ Who
proph - et bards _____ fore - told, _____ When

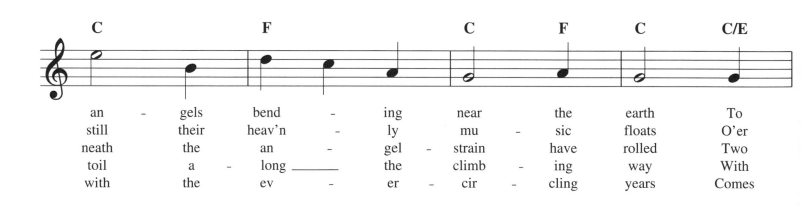

an - gels bend - ing near the earth To
still their heav'n - ly mu - sic floats O'er
neath the an - gel - strain have rolled Two
toil a - long _____ the climb - ing way With
with the ev - er - cir - cling years Comes

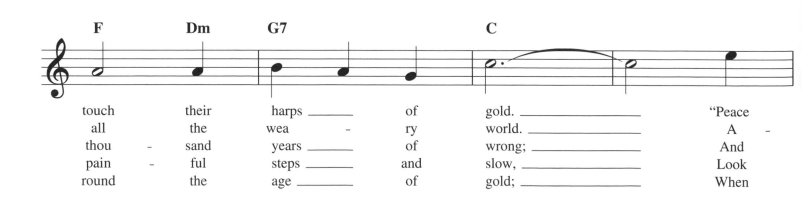

touch their harps _____ of gold. _____ "Peace
all the wea - ry world. _____ A -
thou - sand years _____ of wrong; _____ And
pain - ful steps _____ and slow, _____ Look
round the age _____ of gold; _____ When

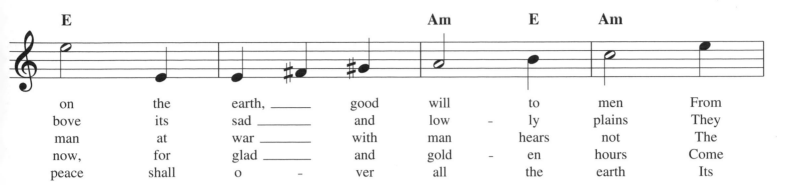

on	the	earth, _____	good	will	to	men	From
bove	its	sad _____	and	low	- ly	plains	They
man	at	war _____	with	man	hears	not	The
now,	for	glad _____	and	gold	- en	hours	Come
peace	shall	o	- ver	all	the	earth	Its

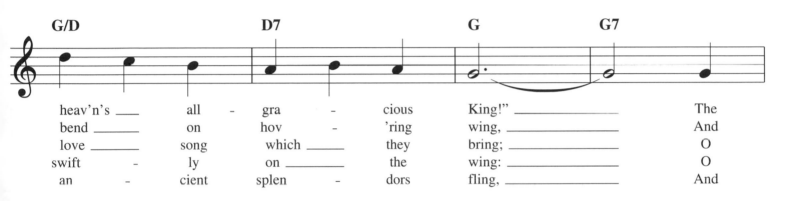

heav'n's ___	all	- gra	- cious	King!" _____	The
bend _____	on	hov	- 'ring	wing, _____	And
love _____	song	which _____	they	bring; _____	O
swift	- ly	on _____	the	wing: _____	O
an	- cient	splen	- dors	fling, _____	And

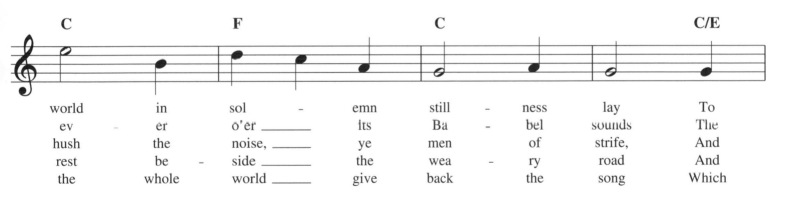

world	in	sol	- emn	still	- ness	lay	To
ev	- er	o'er _____	its	Ba	- bel	sounds	The
hush	the	noise, _____	ye	men	of	strife,	And
rest	be	- side _____	the	wea	- ry	road	And
the	whole	world _____	give	back	the	song	Which

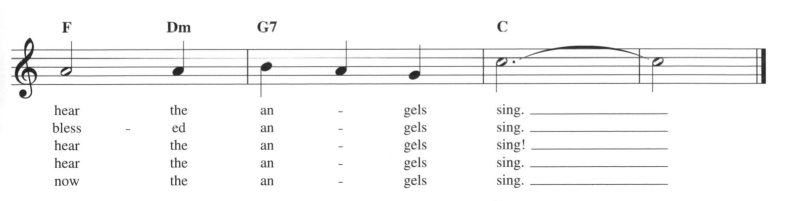

hear	the	an	- gels	sing. _____
bless	- ed	an	- gels	sing. _____
hear	the	an	- gels	sing! _____
hear	the	an	- gels	sing. _____
now	the	an	- gels	sing. _____

IT MUST HAVE BEEN THE MISTLETOE
(Our First Christmas)

By JUSTIN WILDE
and DOUG KONECKY

Moderately

It must have been ___ the mis-tle-toe, ___ the la-zy fire, ___ the
must have been ___ the mis-tle-toe, ___ the la-zy fire, ___ the

fall-ing snow, _ the mag-ic in ___ the frost-y air, ___ that feel-ing
fall-ing snow, _ the mag-ic in ___ the frost-y air, ___ that made me

ev-'ry-where.   It must have been ___ the pret-ty lights _ that glis-tened ___ in the
love   you.   On Christ-mas Eve ___ a wish came true, ___ that night I ___ fell in

si-lent night, _ or may-be just ___ the stars so bright _ that shined a-
love with you. ___ It on-ly took ___ one kiss to know, _ it

bove   you.   Our   first   Christ-mas,   more than _ we'd been dream-ing of. _

_____ Old   Saint   Nich-'las   had his fin-gers crossed, _

___ that we would fall in love. ___ It could have been ___ the

hol-i-day, ___ the mid-night ride ___ up-on a sleigh, ___ the

IT'S BEGINNING TO LOOK LIKE CHRISTMAS

By MEREDITH WILLSON

It's be - gin - ning to look a lot like Christ - mas,

ev - 'ry - where you go. { Take a / There's a

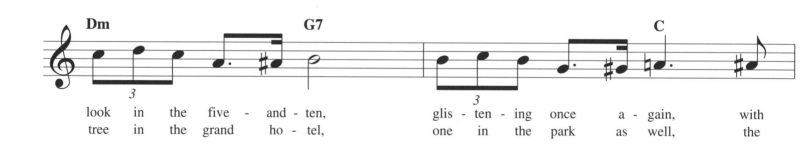

look in the five - and - ten, glis - ten - ing once a - gain, with
tree in the grand ho - tel, one in the park as well, with the

can - dy canes and sil - ver lanes a - glow. It's be -
stur - dy kind that does - n't mind the snow.

gin - ning to look a lot like Christ - mas,

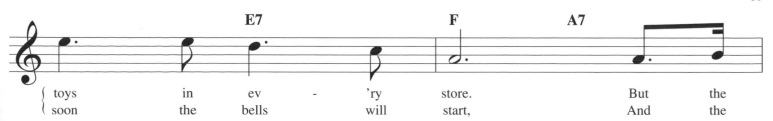

E7   **F**   **A7**

toys   in   ev - 'ry   store.   But   the
soon   the   bells   will   start,   And   the

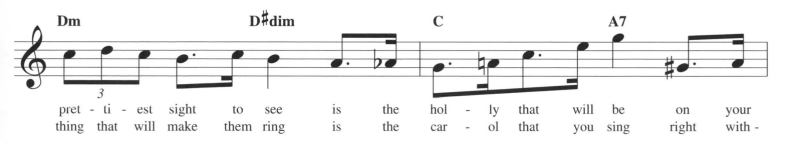

Dm   **D♯dim**   **C**   **A7**

pret - ti - est   sight   to   see   is   the   hol - ly   that   will   be   on   your
thing   that   will   make   them   ring   is   the   car - ol   that   you   sing   right   with -

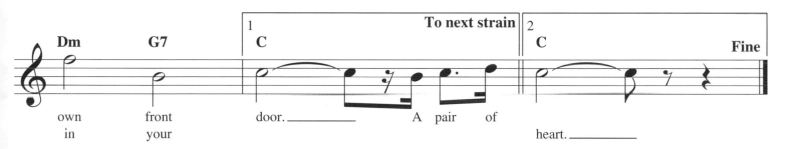

Dm   **G7**   *1* **C**   **To next strain**   *2* **C**   **Fine**

own   front   door._____   A   pair   of
in   your   heart._____

E7   **Am**   **E7**   **Am**

Hop - a - long   boots   and   a   pis - tol   that   shoots   is   the   wish   of   Bar - ney   and   Ben.

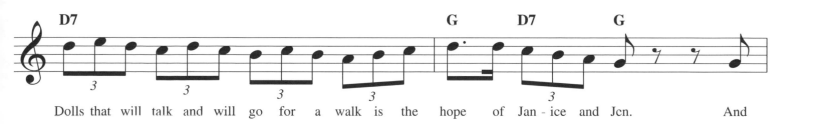

D7   **G**   **D7**   **G**

Dolls   that   will   talk   and   will   go   for   a   walk   is   the   hope   of   Jan - ice   and   Jen.   And

G7   **D.S. al Fine**

Mom   and   Dad   can   hard - ly   wait   for   school   to   start   a - gain.   It's   be -

JINGLE-BELL ROCK

Words and Music by JOE BEAL
and JIM BOOTHE

Moderately

Jin - gle -bell,   jin - gle -bell,   Jin - gle - Bell   Rock   jin - gle bells swing and

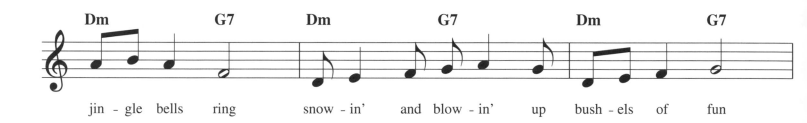

jin - gle bells   ring   snow - in'   and   blow - in'   up   bush - els   of   fun

Now the   jin - gle -hop   has   be - gun.   Jin - gle -bell,   jin - gle -bell,

Jin - gle - Bell   Rock   jin - gle bells chime   in   jin - gle - bell   time,

danc - in'   and   pranc - in'   in   Jin - gle -bell   Square   in the frost - y

air.   What a   bright ___   time ___   it's the   right ___   time ___   to

rock   the   night a -   way,   jin - gle - bell ___   time ___   is a

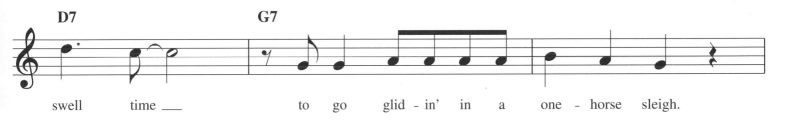

swell   time ___   to go   glid - in'   in   a   one - horse   sleigh.

Gid - dy - up,   jin - gle -horse   pick   up   your   feet   jin - gle   a - round   the

clock;   Mix   and   min -gle   in   a   jin - gl - in'   beat   that's the   Jin - gle - Bell

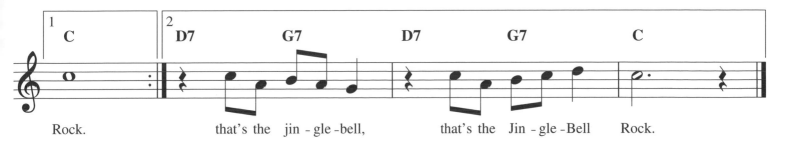

Rock.   that's the   jin - gle -bell,   that's the   Jin - gle -Bell   Rock.

JINGLE BELLS

Words and Music by
J. PIERPONT

Dash - ing thru the snow, In a one - horse o - pen sleigh,
Bells on bob - tail ring, _____ Mak - ing spir - its bright, what

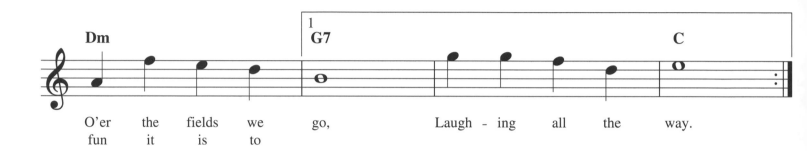

O'er the fields we go, Laugh - ing all the way.
fun it is to

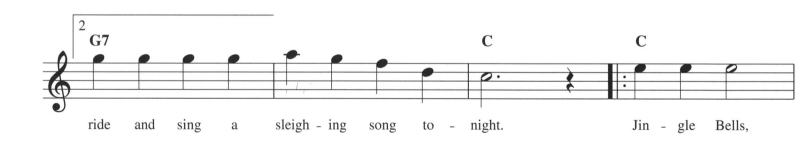

ride and sing a sleigh - ing song to - night. Jin - gle Bells,

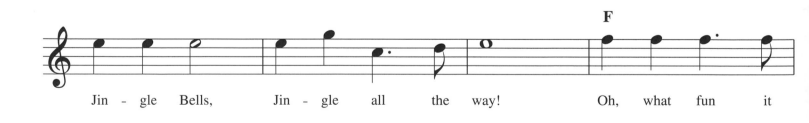

Jin - gle Bells, Jin - gle all the way! Oh, what fun it

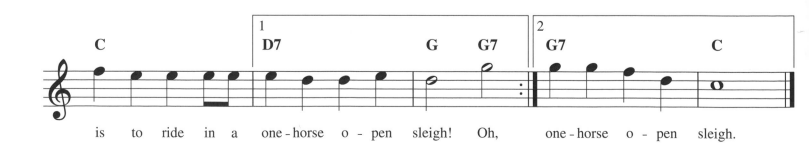

is to ride in a one - horse o - pen sleigh! Oh, one - horse o - pen sleigh.

JOLLY OLD ST. NICHOLAS

Traditional 19th Century American Carol

Lively

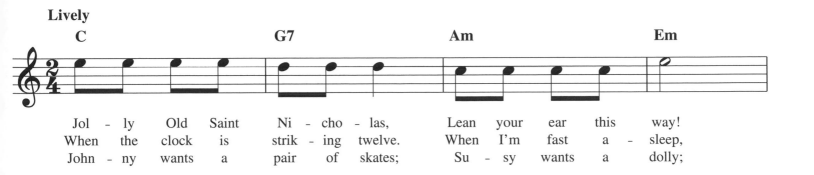

Jol - ly   Old   Saint   Ni - cho - las,   Lean   your   ear   this   way!
When   the   clock   is   strik - ing   twelve.   When   I'm   fast   a - sleep,
John - ny   wants   a   pair   of   skates;   Su - sy   wants   a   dolly;

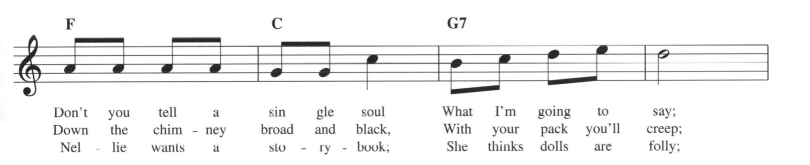

Don't   you   tell   a   sin - gle   soul   What   I'm   going   to   say;
Down   the   chim - ney   broad   and   black,   With   your   pack   you'll   creep;
Nel - lie   wants   a   sto - ry - book;   She   thinks   dolls   are   folly;

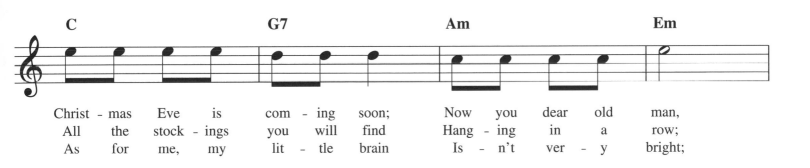

Christ - mas   Eve   is   com - ing   soon;   Now   you   dear   old   man,
All   the   stock - ings   you   will   find   Hang - ing   in   a   row;
As   for   me,   my   lit - tle   brain   Is - n't   ver - y   bright;

Whis - per   what   you'll   bring   to   me;   Tell   me   if   you   can.
Mine   will   be   the   short - est   one,   You'll   be   sure   to   know.
Choose   for   me,   old   San - ta   Claus,   What   you   think   is   right.

JOY TO THE WORLD

Words by ISAAC WATTS
Music by GEORGE FRIDERIC HANDEL
Arranged by LOWELL MASON

LAST CHRISTMAS

Words and Music by
GEORGE MICHAEL

Slowly and freely

Last Christ - mas I gave you my heart, __ but the ver - y next day you

gave it a - way. __ This year __ to save me from tears __ I'll

give it to some - one spe - cial.   - cial.

To Coda   1, 3, 5   2, 4

(Instrumental)

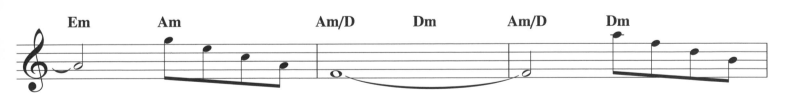

Once   bit - ten   and
A   crowd - ed   room,

twice shy, _____ I keep my dis - tance but
friends with tired _____ eyes. _____ I'm hid - ing from you

tears still catch _____ my eye. _____ Tell me, ba - by,
and your soul _____ of ice. _____ My god, I thought you were

do you rec - og - nize _____ me? Well, it's been a year. _____ It
some - one to re - ly _____ on. Me, I guess I was a

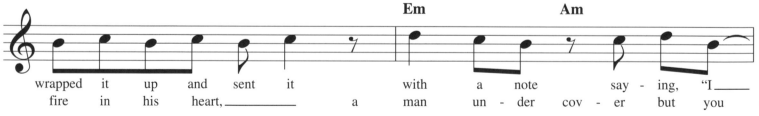

does - n't sur - prise _____ me. Hap - py Christ - mas. I
shoul - der to cry _____ on. A face on a lov - er with a

wrapped it up and sent it with a note say - ing, "I
fire in his heart, _____ a man un - der cov - er but you

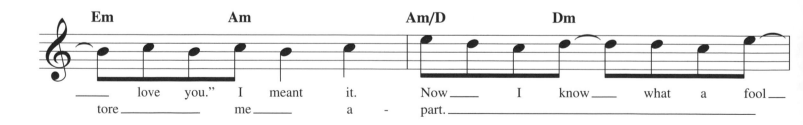

_____ love you." I meant it. Now _____ I know _____ what a fool _____
tore _____ me _____ a - part. _____

_____ I've been. _____ But if you kissed me now _____ I know you'd
Oo, _____ now I've found a real _____ love. You'll nev - er

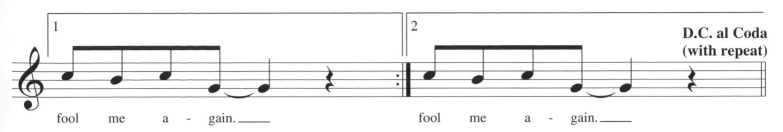

fool me a - gain. _____ fool me a - gain. _____

D.C. al Coda (with repeat)

CODA

\- cial. A face on a lov - er with a

fire in his heart, _____ a man un - der cov - er but you tore him a - part. _____

May - be next year I'll give it to some - one, I'll

give it to some - one spe - cial, spe - cial. _____

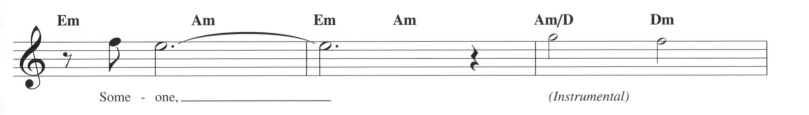

Some - one, _____ *(Instrumental)*

some-one. I'll give it to some - one, I'll give it to some - one spe -

Repeat ad lib. and Fade

LET IT SNOW! LET IT SNOW! LET IT SNOW!

Words by SAMMY CAHN
Music by JULE STYNE

Oh the weath-er out-side is fright-ful But the fire is so de-
does-n't show signs of stop-ping And I brought some corn for
fi-re is slow-ly dy-ing And my dear, we're still good-

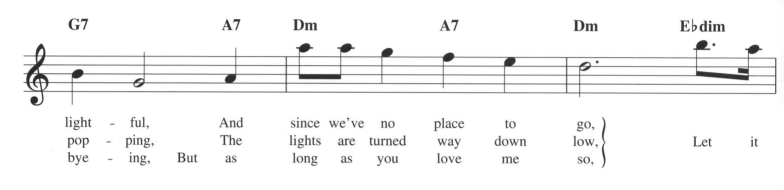

light-ful, And since we've no place to go,
pop-ping, The lights are turned way down low, Let it
bye-ing, But as long as you love me so,

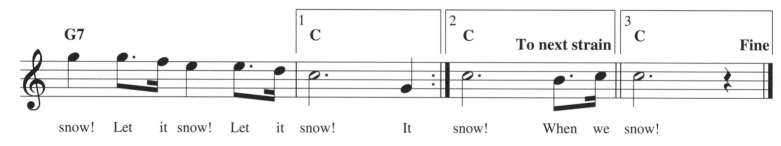

snow! Let it snow! Let it snow! It snow! When we snow!

fi-nal-ly kiss good night How I'll hate go-ing out in the storm! But if

D.S. al Fine

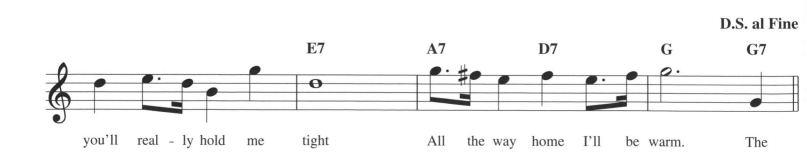

you'll real-ly hold me tight All the way home I'll be warm. The

MELE KALIKIMAKA

Words and Music by
R. ALEX ANDERSON

Me - le Ka - li - ki - ma - ka is the thing to say, _____ on a

bright Ha - wai - ian Christ - mas day. _____

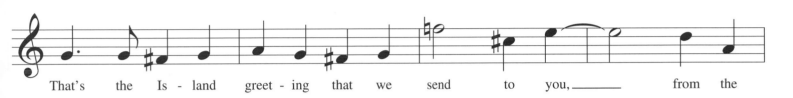

That's the Is - land greet - ing that we send to you, _____ from the

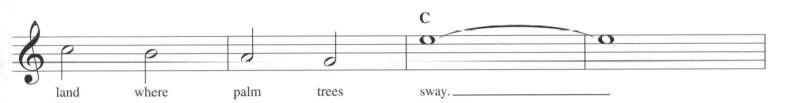

land where palm trees sway. _____

Here we know that Christ - mas will be green and bright, the

sun will shine by day, and all the stars at night.

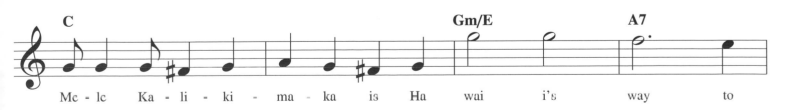

Me - le Ka - li - ki - ma - ka is Ha - wai - i's way to

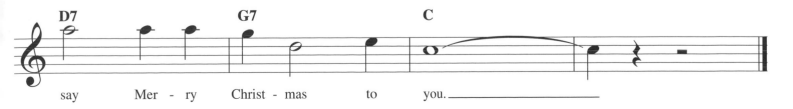

say Mer - ry Christ - mas to you. _____

LITTLE SAINT NICK

Words and Music by BRIAN WILSON
and MIKE LOVE

Well, _____ way up north where the air gets cold, ___ there's a
lit - tle bob - sled, we call it Old Saint Nick, ___ but she'll
haul -in' through the snow at a fright -'nin' speed ___ with a

tale a - bout Christ - mas that you've all been told. ___ And a
walk a to - bog - gan with a four - speed stick. ___ She's
half a doz - en deer ___ with ___ Ru - dy to lead. He's

real fa - mous cat all dressed up in red, _____ and he
can - dy ap - ple red with a ski for a wheel, and when
got - ta wear his gog - gles 'cause the snow real - ly flies, and he's

spends the whole ___ year work - in' out on his sled. ___
San - ta hits the gas, man, just watch her _____ peel. ___ } It's the
cruis - in' ev - 'ry pad with a lit - tle sur - prise. ___

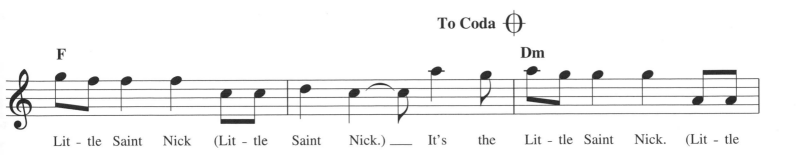

To Coda

Lit - tle Saint Nick (Lit - tle Saint Nick.) ___ It's the Lit - tle Saint Nick. (Lit - tle

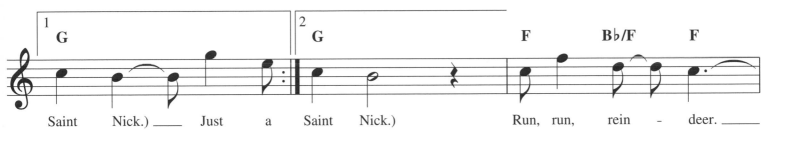

Saint Nick.) ___ Just a Saint Nick.) Run, run, rein - deer. ___

___ Run, run, rein - deer. Oh. ___

Run, run, rein - deer. ___ Run, run, rein - deer. He

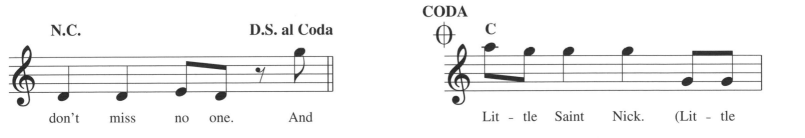

don't miss no one. And

CODA

Lit - tle Saint Nick. (Lit - tle

Saint Nick.) Ah. ___ Mer - ry Christ - mas, Saint ___ Nick. ___

MARCH OF THE TOYS
from BABES IN TOYLAND

By VICTOR HERBERT

A MARSHMALLOW WORLD

Words by CARL SIGMAN
Music by PETER DE ROSE

With motion

It's a marsh - mal - low world in the win - ter_____ when the
marsh - mal - low clouds be - ing friend - ly_____ in the

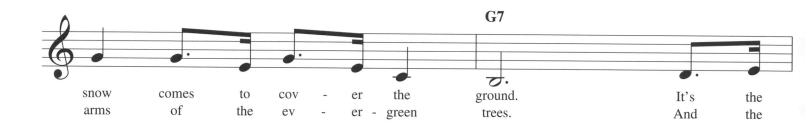

snow comes to cov - er the ground. It's the
arms of the ev - er - green trees. And the

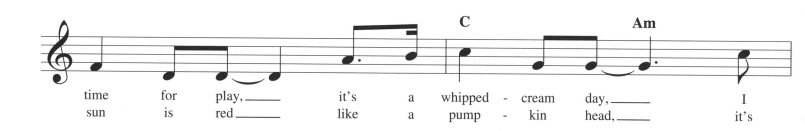

time for play,_____ it's a whipped - cream day,_____ I
sun is red_____ like a pump - kin head,_____ it's

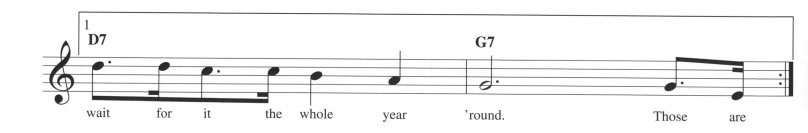

1
wait for it the whole year 'round. Those are

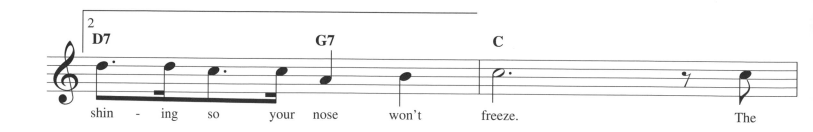

2
shin - ing so your nose won't freeze. The

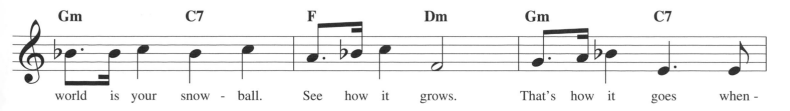

world is your snow - ball. See how it grows. That's how it goes when -

ev - er it snows. The world is your snow - ball

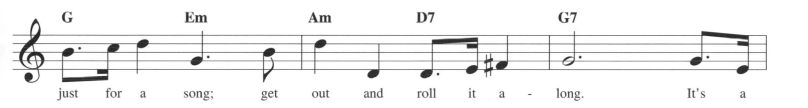

just for a song; get out and roll it a - long. It's a

yum - yum - my world made for sweet - hearts._____ Take a

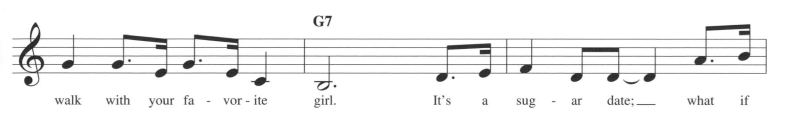

walk with your fa - vor - ite girl. It's a sug - ar date;___ what if

spring is late?___ In win - ter it's a marsh - mal - low world.

MERRY CHRISTMAS, DARLING

Words and Music by RICHARD CARPENTER
and FRANK POOLER

MERRY MERRY CHRISTMAS, BABY

Words and Music by MARGO SYLVIA
and GIL LOPEZ

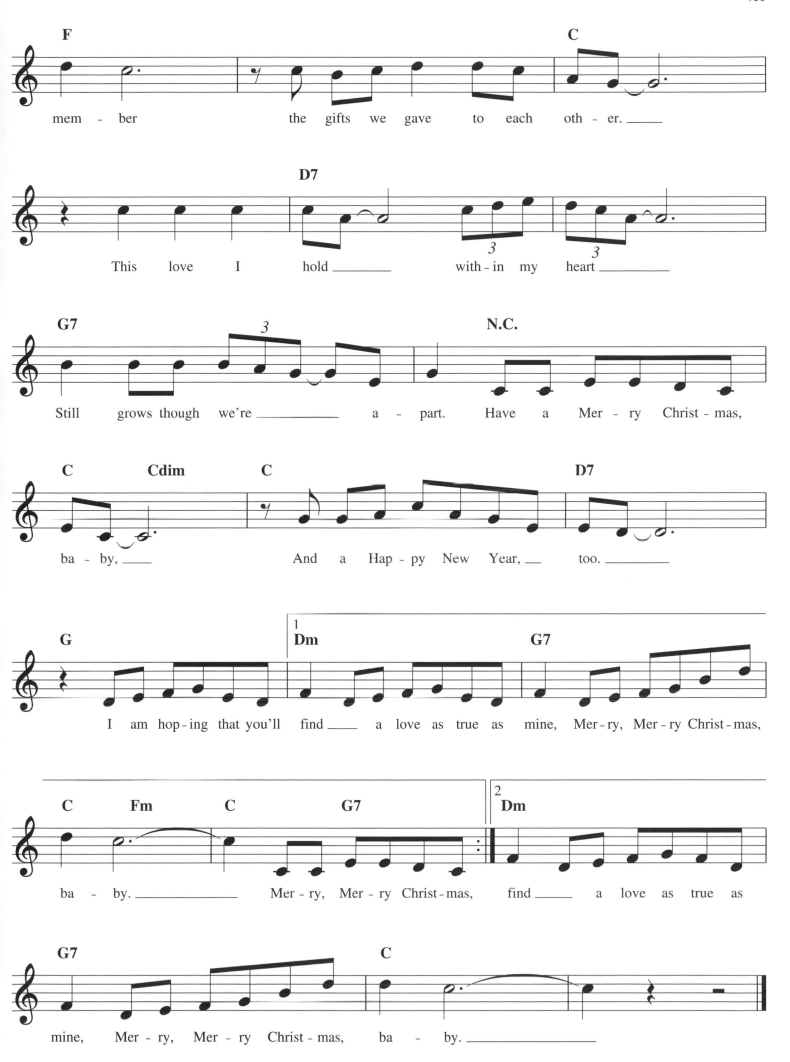

MISTER SANTA

Words and Music by
PAT BALLARD

Additional Verses

2. Mister Santa, dear old Saint Nick
   Be awful careful and please don't get sick
   Put on your coat when breezes are blowin'
   And when you cross the street look where you're goin'.
   Santa, we (I) love you so,
   We (I) hope you never get lost in the snow.
   Take your time when you unpack,
   Mister Santa don't hurry back.

3. Mister Santa, we've been so good
   We've washed the dishes and done what we should.
   Made up the beds and scrubbed up our toesies,
   We've used a kleenex when we've blown our nosies.
   Santa look at our ears, they're clean as whistles,
   We're sharper than shears
   Now we've put you on the spot,
   Mister Santa bring us a lot.

MISTLETOE AND HOLLY

Words and Music by FRANK SINATRA,
DOK STANFORD and HENRY W. SANICOLA

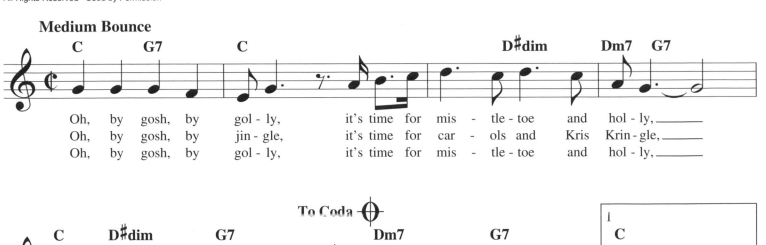

Oh, by gosh, by gol - ly, it's time for mis - tle - toe and hol - ly,
Oh, by gosh, by jin - gle, it's time for car - ols and Kris Krin - gle,
Oh, by gosh, by gol - ly, it's time for mis - tle - toe and hol - ly,

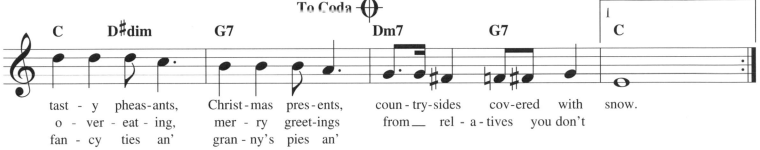

tast - y pheas - ants, Christ - mas pres - ents, coun - try - sides cov - ered with snow.
o - ver - eat - ing, mer - ry greet - ings from rel - a - tives you don't
fan - cy ties an' gran - ny's pies an'

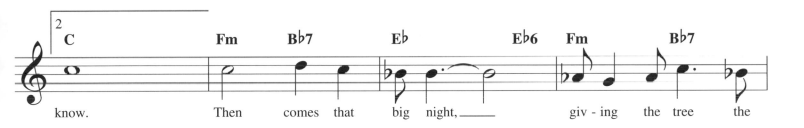

know. Then comes that big night, giv - ing the tree the

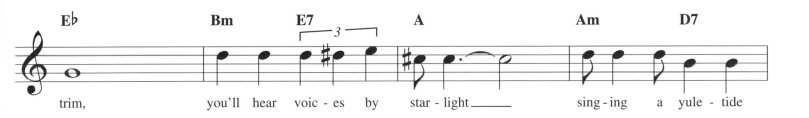

trim, you'll hear voic - es by star - light sing - ing a yule - tide

hymn.   folks steal - in' a kiss or two   as they

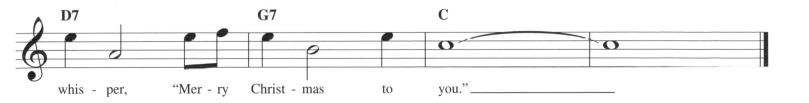

whis - per, "Mer - ry Christ - mas to you." _____

THE MOST WONDERFUL TIME OF THE YEAR

Words and Music by EDDIE POLA
and GEORGE WYLE

Brightly, in one

It's the most won - der - ful time___ of the
hap - hap - pi - est sea - son of
most won - der - ful time___ of the

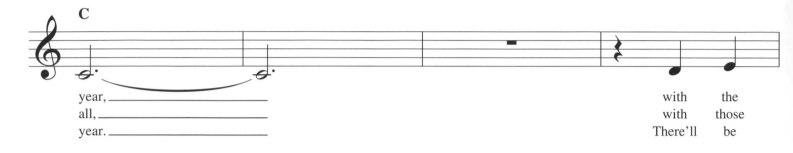

year,_____ with the
all,_____ with those
year._____ There'll be

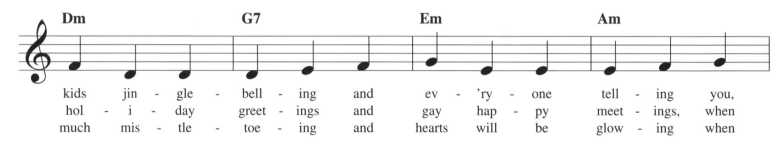

kids jin - gle - bell - ing and ev - 'ry - one tell - ing you,
hol - i - day greet - ings and gay hap - py meet - ings, when
much mis - tle - toe - ing and gay hearts will be glow - ing when

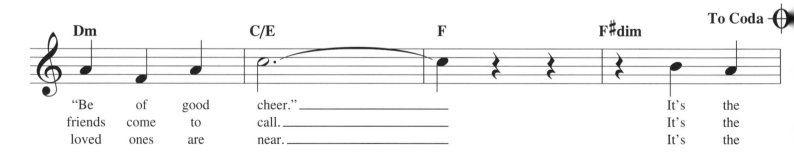

"Be of good cheer."_____ It's the
friends come to call._____ It's the
loved ones are near._____ It's the

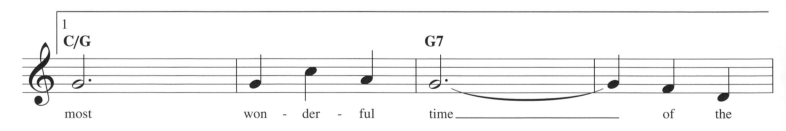

most won - der - ful time_____ of the

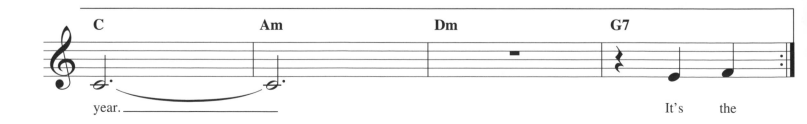

year._____ It's the

MY FAVORITE THINGS
from THE SOUND OF MUSIC

Lyrics by OSCAR HAMMERSTEIN II
Music by RICHARD RODGERS

Moderately

Rain - drops on ros - es and whis - kers on kit - tens,
Cream col - ored po - nies and crisp ap - ple strud - els,

bright cop - per ket - tles and warm wool - en mit - tens,
door - bells and sleigh - bells and schnitz - el with noo - dles,

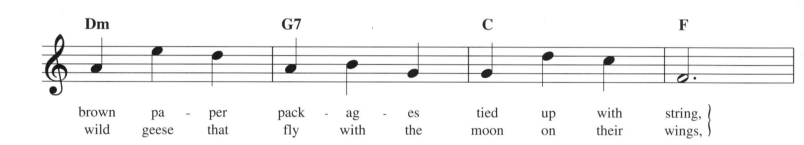

brown pa - per pack - ag - es tied up with string, }
wild geese that fly with the moon on their wings, }

these are a few of my fa - vor - ite things.

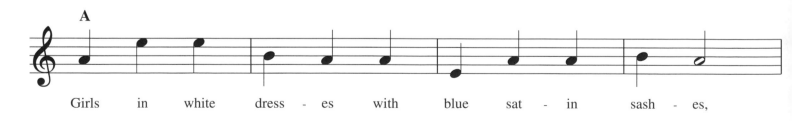

Girls in white dress - es with blue sat - in sash - es,

snow - flakes that stay on my nose and eye - lash - es,

NOT THAT FAR FROM BETHLEHEM

Words and Music by JEFF BORDERS,
GAYLA BORDERS and LOWELL ALEXANDER

O CHRISTMAS TREE

Traditional German Carol

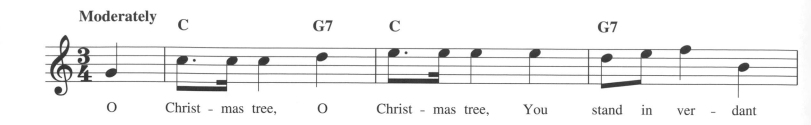

O   Christ - mas tree,   O   Christ - mas tree,   You   stand   in   ver - dant

beau   - ty!   O   Christ - mas tree,   O   Christ - mas tree,   You

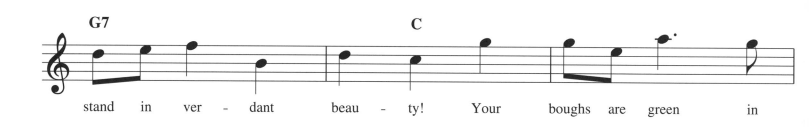

stand   in   ver - dant   beau - ty!   Your   boughs   are   green   in

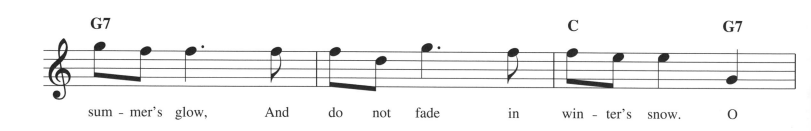

sum - mer's   glow,   And   do   not   fade   in   win - ter's   snow.   O

Christ - mas tree,   O   Christ - mas tree,   You   stand   in   ver - dant   beau - ty!

O COME, ALL YE FAITHFUL
(Adeste fideles)

Words and Music by JOHN FRANCIS WADE
Latin Words translated by FREDERICK OAKELEY

Moderately

A - des - te, fi - de - les,   lae - ti tri - um - phan - tes, Ve -
O   come,   all ye faith - ful,   Joy - ful and tri - um - phant, O
Sing,   choirs of an - gels,   Sing in ex - ul - ta - tion, ____
Yea,   Lord,   we greet Thee,   Born this hap - py morn - ing; ____

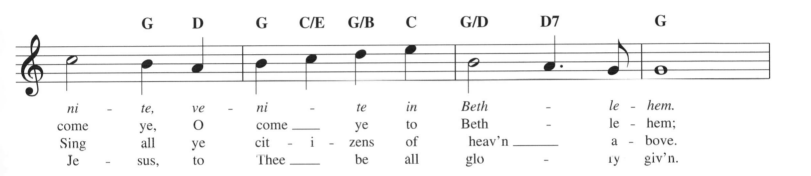

ni - te,   ve - ni - te   in Beth - le - hem.
come ye,   O come ____ ye to Beth - le - hem;
Sing all ye cit - i - zens of heav'n _____ a - bove.
Je - sus, to Thee ____ be all glo - ry giv'n.

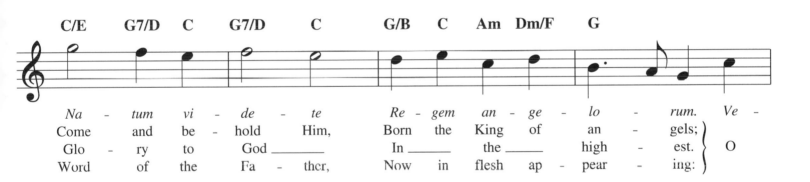

Na - tum vi - de - te   Re - gem an - ge - lo - rum. Ve -
Come and be - hold Him,   Born the King of an - gels; ⎫
Glo - ry to God _____   In _____ the _____ high - est. ⎬ O
Word of the Fa - ther,   Now in flesh ap - pear - ing: ⎭

ni - te a - do - re - mus, ve - ni - te a - do - re - mus, ve -
come let us a - dore Him, O come let us a - dore Him, O

ni - te a - do - re - mus ____ Do - mi - num.
come let us a - dore Him, ____ Christ ____ the Lord.

O COME, O COME, IMMANUEL

Plainsong, 13th Century
Words translated by JOHN M. NEALE
and HENRY S. COFFIN

O HOLY NIGHT

French Words by PLACIDE CAPPEAU
English Words by JOHN S. DWIGHT
Music by ADOLPHE ADAM

Moderately

O LITTLE TOWN OF BETHLEHEM

Words by PHILLIPS BROOKS
Music by LEWIS H. REDNER

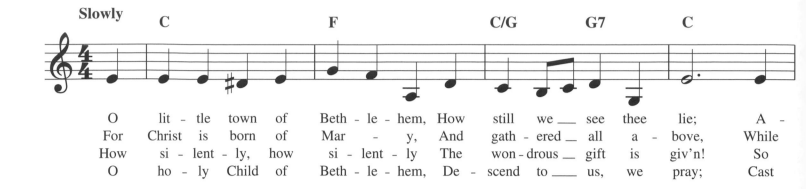

O   lit - tle   town   of   Beth - le - hem,   How   still   we __ see   thee   lie;   A -
For   Christ   is   born   of   Mar   -   y,   And   gath - ered __ all   a - bove,   While
How   si - lent - ly,   how   si - lent - ly   The   won - drous __ gift   is   giv'n!   So
O   ho - ly   Child   of   Beth - le - hem,   De - scend   to ___ us,   we   pray;   Cast

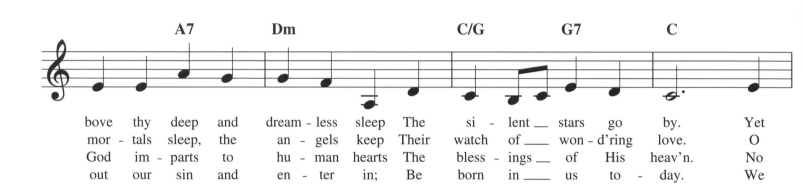

bove   thy   deep   and   dream - less   sleep   The   si - lent __ stars   go   by.   Yet
mor - tals   sleep,   the   an - gels   keep   Their   watch   of ___ won - d'ring   love.   O
God   im - parts   to   hu - man   hearts   The   bless - ings __ of   His   heav'n.   No
out   our   sin   and   en - ter   in;   Be   born   in ___ us   to - day.   We

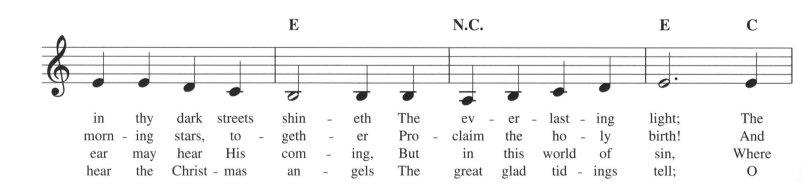

in   thy   dark   streets   shin - eth   The   ev - er - last - ing   light;   The
morn - ing   stars,   to - geth - er   Pro - claim   the   ho - ly   birth!   And
ear   may   hear   His   com - ing,   But   in   this   world   of   sin,   Where
hear   the   Christ - mas   an - gels   The   great   glad   tid - ings   tell;   O

hopes   and   fears   of   all   the   years   Are   met   in   thee   to - night.
prais - es   sing   to   God   the   King,   And   peace   to   men   on   earth.
meek   souls   will   re - ceive   Him   still,   The   dear   Christ   en - ters   in.
come   to   us,   a - bide   with   us,   Our   Lord   Em - man - u - el!

ONCE IN ROYAL DAVID'S CITY

Words by CECIL F. ALEXANDER
Music by HENRY J. GAUNTLETT

Moderately

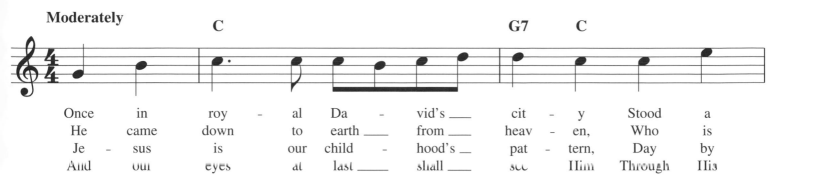

Once in roy - al Da - vid's ___ cit - y Stood a
He came down to earth ___ from ___ heav - en, Who is
Je - sus is our child - hood's _ pat - tern, Day by
And our eyes at last ___ shall ___ see Him Through His

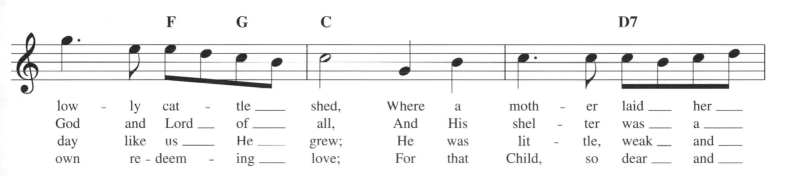

low - ly cat - tle ___ shed, Where a moth - er laid ___ her ___
God and Lord __ of ___ all, And His shel - ter was ___ a ___
day like us ___ He ___ grew; He was lit - tle, weak __ and ___
own re - deem - ing ___ love; For that Child, so dear ___ and ___

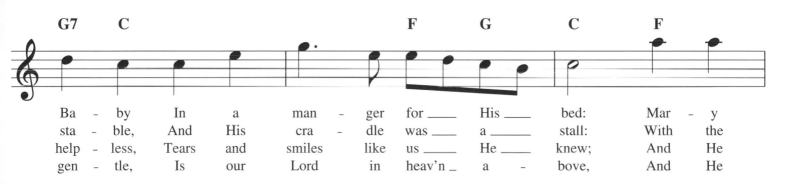

Ba - by In a man - ger for ___ His ___ bed: Mar - y
sta - ble, And His cra - dle was ___ a ___ stall: With the
help - less, Tears and smiles like us ___ He ___ knew; And He
gen - tle, Is our Lord in heav'n _ a - bove, And He

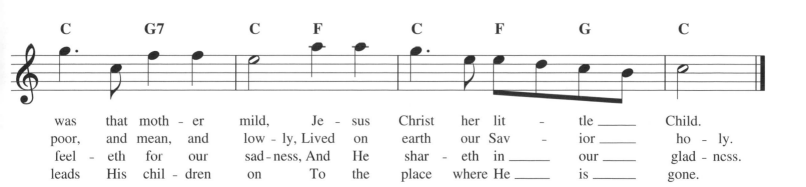

was that moth - er mild, Je - sus Christ her lit - tle ___ Child.
poor, and mean, and low - ly, Lived on earth our Sav - ior ___ ho - ly.
feel - eth for our sad - ness, And He shar - eth in ___ our ___ glad - ness.
leads His chil - dren on To the place where He ___ is ___ gone.

ROCKIN' AROUND THE CHRISTMAS TREE

Music and Lyrics by
JOHNNY MARKS

Lively

Rock-in' a - round the Christ - mas tree ___ at the Christ - mas par - ty hop, ___

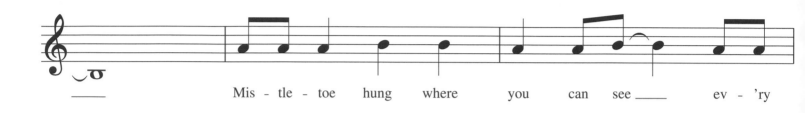

___ Mis - tle - toe hung where you can see ___ ev - 'ry

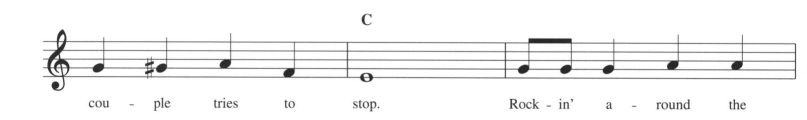

cou - ple tries to stop. Rock - in' a - round the

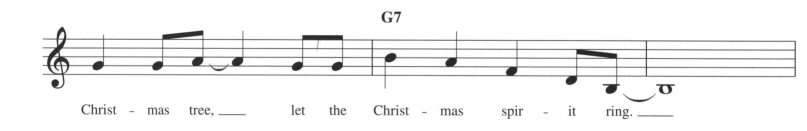

Christ - mas tree, ___ let the Christ - mas spir - it ring. ___

Lat - er we'll have some pun - kin pie ___ and we'll do some car - ol -

ing. You will get a sen - ti - men - tal

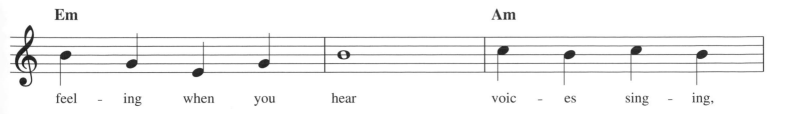

Em   **Am**

feel - ing   when   you   hear   voic - es   sing - ing,

                        D7   **G7**

"Let's   be   jol - ly.   Deck   the   halls   with   boughs   of   hol - ly."

C   **G7**

Rock-in'   a - round   the   Christ - mas   tree. ___   Have   a   hap   py   hol   i   day. _

___   Ev - 'ry - one   danc - ing   mer - ri - ly ____   in   the

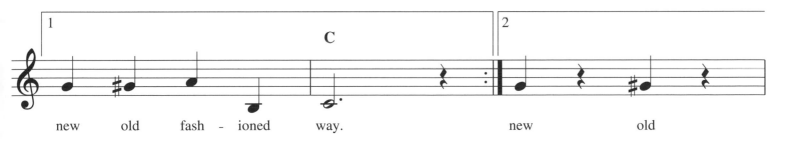

1   **C**   2

new   old   fash - ioned   way.   new   old

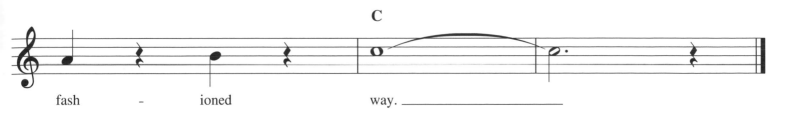

                        C

fash - ioned   way. _____

RUDOLPH THE RED-NOSED REINDEER

Music and Lyrics by
JOHNNY MARKS

You know Dash - er and Danc - er and Pranc - er and Vix - en,

Com - et and Cu - pid and Don - ner and Blitz - en, but do you re -

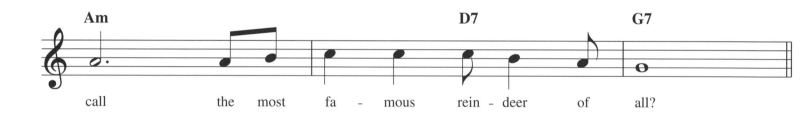

call the most fa - mous rein - deer of all?

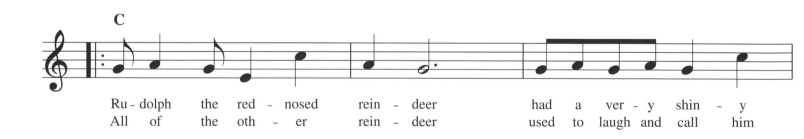

Ru - dolph the red - nosed rein - deer had a ver - y shin - y
All of the oth - er rein - deer used to laugh and call him

nose, and if you ev - er saw it,
names, they nev - er let poor Ru - dolph

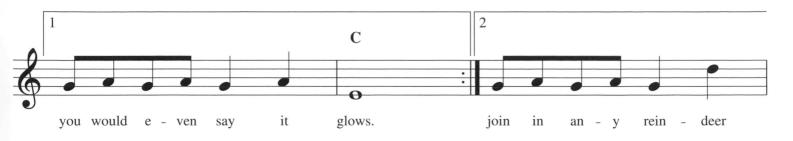

you would e - ven say it glows. join in an - y rein - deer

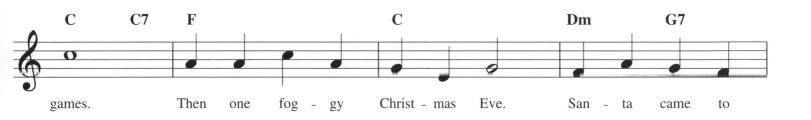

games. Then one fog - gy Christ - mas Eve. San - ta came to

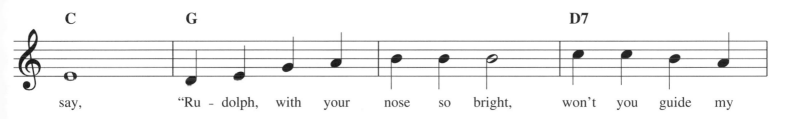

say, "Ru - dolph, with your nose so bright, won't you guide my

sleigh to - night?"__ Then how the rein - deer loved him

as they shout - ed out with glee: "Ru - dolph the red - nosed

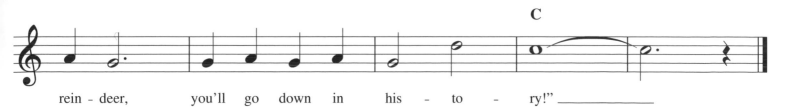

rein - deer, you'll go down in his - to - ry!"_____

SANTA BABY

By JOAN JAVITS, PHIL SPRINGER
and TONY SPRINGER

SANTA CLAUS IS COMIN' TO TOWN

Words by HAVEN GILLESPIE
Music by J. FRED COOTS

SILENT NIGHT

Words by JOSEPH MOHR
Translated by JOHN F. YOUNG
Music by FRANZ X. GRUBER

SHAKE ME I RATTLE
(Squeeze Me I Cry)

Words and Music by HAL HACKADY
and CHARLES NAYLOR

Moderately slow

I was pass - ing by a toy shop on the
called an - oth - er toy shop on a
late and snow was fall - ing as the

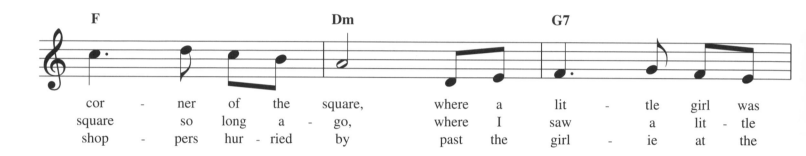

cor - ner of the square, where a lit - tle girl was
square so long a - go, where I saw a lit - tle
shop - pers hur - ried by past the girl - ie at the

look - ing in the win - dow there. She was
dol - ly that I want - ed so. I re -
win - dow with her lit - tle head held high. They were

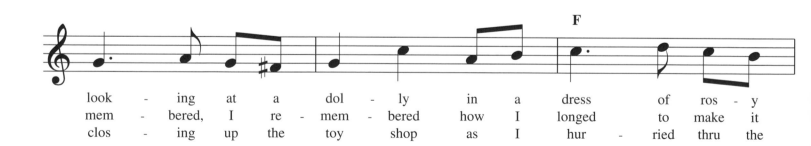

look - ing at a dol - ly in a dress of ros - y
mem - bered, I re - mem - bered how I longed to make it
clos - ing up the toy shop as I hur - ried thru the

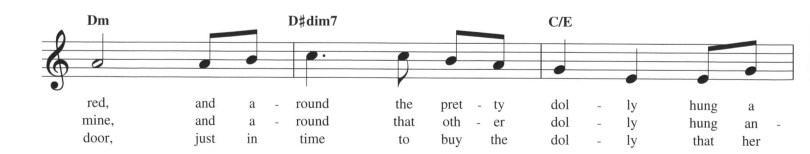

red, and a - round the pret - ty dol - ly hung a
mine, and a - round that oth - er dol - ly hung an -
door, just in time to buy the dol - ly that her

SILVER BELLS
from the Paramount Picture THE LEMON DROP KID

Words and Music by JAY LIVINGSTON
and RAY EVANS

SNOWFALL

Lyrics by RUTH THORNHILL
Music by CLAUDE THORNHILL

SOMEWHERE IN MY MEMORY
from the Twentieth Century Fox Motion Picture HOME ALONE

Words by LESLIE BRICUSSE
Music by JOHN WILLIAMS

Gently and with simplicity

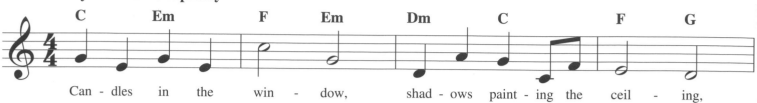

Can - dles in the win - dow, shad - ows paint - ing the ceil - ing,

gaz - ing at the fire glow, feel - ing that "gin - ger - bread"

feel - ing. Pre - cious mo - ments, spe - cial peo - ple,

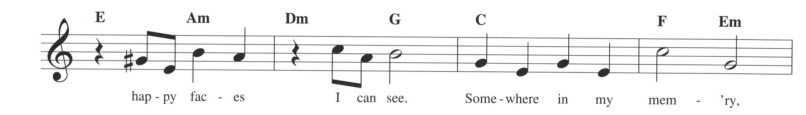

hap - py fac - es I can see. Some - where in my mem - 'ry,

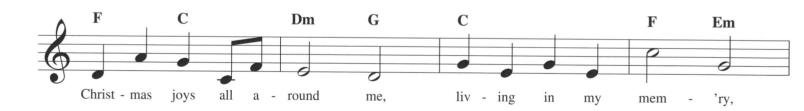

Christ - mas joys all a - round me, liv - ing in my mem - 'ry,

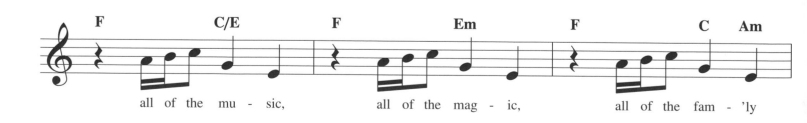

all of the mu - sic, all of the mag - ic, all of the fam - 'ly

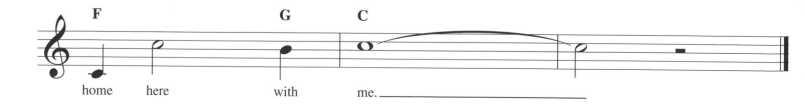

home here with me.

STILL, STILL, STILL

Salzburg Melody, c.1819
Traditional Austrian Text

Gently

Still, _____ still, _____ still,   To _____ sleep is _____ now His _____
Sleep, _____ sleep, _____ sleep,   While _ we Thy _____ vi - gil _____

will.   On Mar - y's _____ breast He rests in _____ slum - ber,
keep.   And an - gels _____ come from Heav - en sing - ing,

While we _____ pray in end - less _____ num - ber,   Still, _____ still, _____
Songs of ju - bi - la - tion _____ bring - ing,   Sleep, _____ sleep, _____

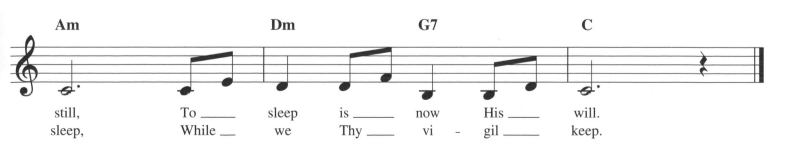

still,   To _____ sleep is _____ now His _____ will.
sleep,   While _ we Thy _____ vi - gil _____ keep.

SUSSEX CAROL

Traditional English Carol

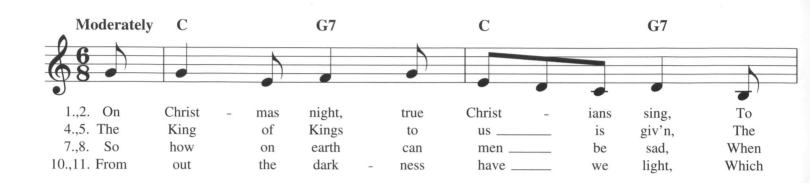

	On	Christ - mas	night,	true	Christ - ians	sing,	To
1.,2.							
4.,5. The	King	of	Kings	to	us _____	is	giv'n,	The
7.,8. So	how	on	earth	can	men _____	be	sad,	When
10.,11. From	out	the	dark - ness	have _____	we	light,	Which

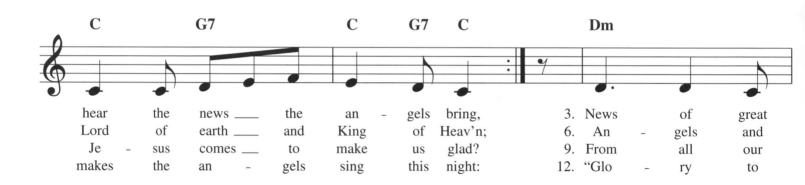

hear the news ____ the an - gels bring,   3. News of great
Lord of earth ____ and King of Heav'n;   6. An - gels and
Je - sus comes ____ to make us glad?   9. From all our
makes the an - gels sing this night: 12. "Glo - ry to

joy _____ and of _____ great mirth,   Tid - ings
men _____ with joy _____ may sing   Of blest
sins _____ to set _____ us free,   Buy - ing
God, _____ His peace ____ to men,   And good

of our dear Sav - ior's birth. _____
Je - sus, their new - born King. _____
for us our lib - er - ty. _____
will, ev - er - more! ____ A - men." _____

SUZY SNOWFLAKE

Words and Music by SID TEPPER
and ROY BENNETT

THIS CHRISTMAS

Words and Music by DONNY HATHAWAY
and NADINE McKINNOR

Moderately

(1.,4.) Hang all the mis-tle-toe.____ I'm gon-na get to know you
(2.) Pres-ents and cards are here.____ My world is filled with cheer and
(3.) *Piano solo ad lib.*

bet - ter____ this Christ - mas.
you____ this Christ - mas.

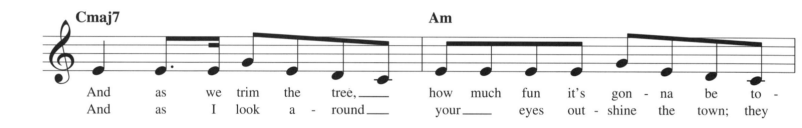

And as we trim the tree,____ how much fun it's gon-na be to -
And as I look a - round____ your____ eyes out - shine the town; they

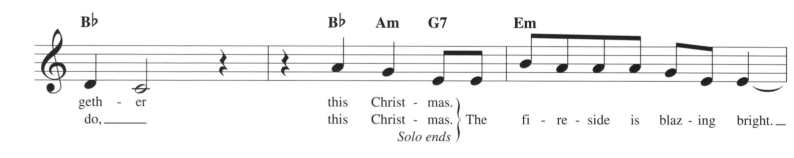

geth - er this Christ - mas.}
do,____ this Christ - mas.} The fi - re - side is blaz-ing bright.____
Solo ends

____ We're car - ol - in' through the night____ and this

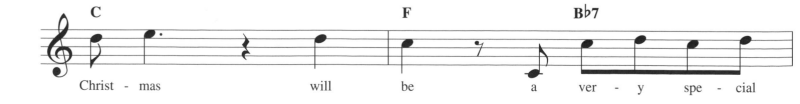

Christ - mas will be a ver - y spe - cial

THE TWELVE DAYS OF CHRISTMAS

Traditional English Carol

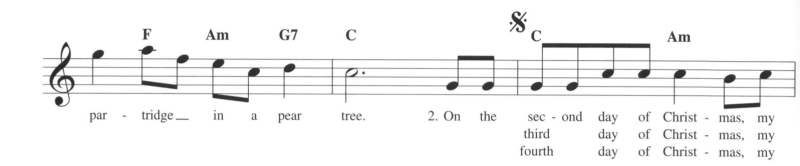

1. On the first day of Christ - mas, my true love sent to me: A par - tridge__ in a pear tree. 2. On the sec - ond day of Christ - mas, my
third day of Christ - mas, my
fourth day of Christ - mas, my

Repeat as needed

true love sent to me: two tur - tle - doves
true love sent to me: three French__ hens, and a par - tridge__ in a pear
true love sent to me: four call - ing birds,

D.S. for Vs. 3 and 4

tree. 3.,4. On the tree. 5. On the fifth day of Christ - mas, my

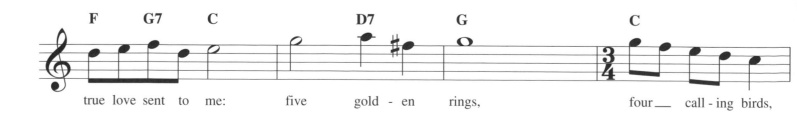

true love sent to me: five gold - en rings, four__ call - ing birds,

three French hens, two___ tur - tle - doves and a par - tridge___ in a pear

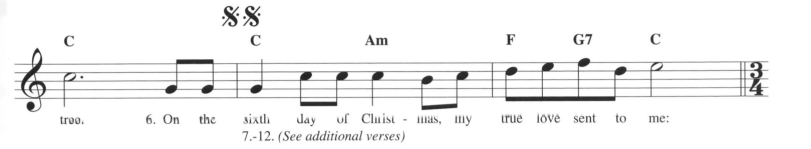

troo. 6. On the sixth day of Christ - mas, my true love sent to me:
7.-12. *(See additional verses)*

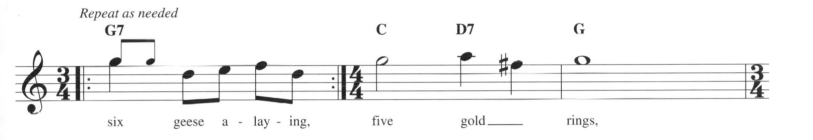

Repeat as needed

six geese a - lay - ing, five gold___ rings,

four___ call - ing birds, three French hens, two___ tur - tle - doves and a

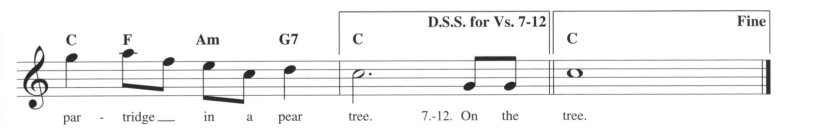

par - tridge___ in a pear tree. 7.-12. On the tree.

Additional Verses

On the seventh day ... seven swans a-swimming
On the eighth day ... eight maids a-milking
On the ninth day ... nine ladies dancing
On the tenth day ... ten lords a-leaping
On the eleventh day ... 'leven Pipers piping
On the twelfth day ... twelve drummers drummming

UP ON THE HOUSETOP

Words and Music by
B.R. HANDY

Moderately

Up   on   the house - top ___ rein - deer pause,   Out jumps good old
First comes the stock - ing of lit - tle Nell;   Oh, dear San - ta,
Next comes the stock - ing of lit - tle Will;   Oh, just see what a

San - ta Claus;   Down thro' the chim - ney with lots of toys,
fill it well;   Give her a dol - lie that laughs and cries,
glo - rious fill!   Here is a ham - mer and lots of tacks,

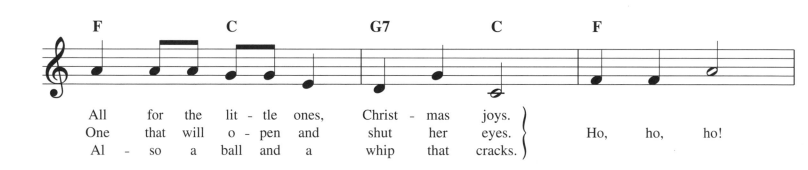

All for the lit - tle ones,   Christ - mas joys.   Ho, ho, ho!
One that will o - pen and shut her eyes.
Al - so a ball and a whip that cracks.

who would - n't go!   Ho, ho, ho!   who would - n't go! ___

Up on the house - top, click, click, click.   Down thro' the chim - ney with good Saint Nick.

WASSAIL, WASSAIL

Old English Air

Moderately

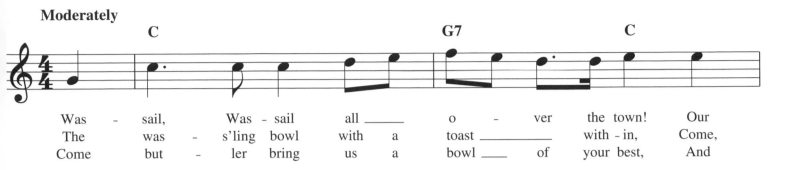

Was - sail, Was - sail all _____ o - ver the town! Our
The was - s'ling bowl with a toast _____ with - in, Come,
Come but - ler bring us a bowl ____ of your best, And

bread it is white and our ale it is brown; Our
fill it up now un - to _____ the brim. Come,
we hope your soul in _____ heav - en shall rest. But

bowl is made of the ma - ple tree, So
fill it up that we may _____ all see, With the
if you bring us a bowl ____ too small, Then

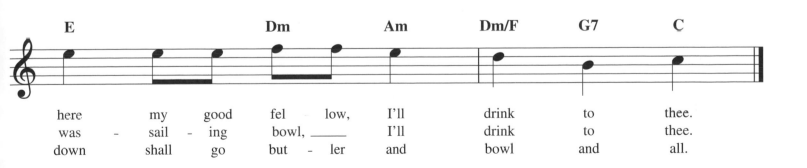

here my good fel - low, I'll drink to thee.
was - sail - ing bowl, _____ I'll drink to thee.
down shall go but - ler and bowl and all.

WE THREE KINGS OF ORIENT ARE

Words and Music by
JOHN H. HOPKINS, JR.

WE WISH YOU A MERRY CHRISTMAS

Traditional English Folksong

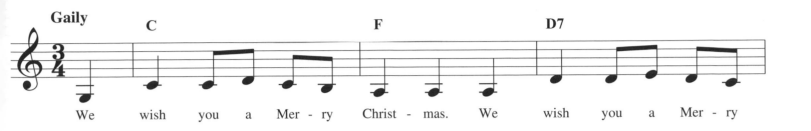

We wish you a Mer - ry Christ - mas. We wish you a Mer - ry

Christ - mas. We wish you a Mer - ry Christ - mas, and a

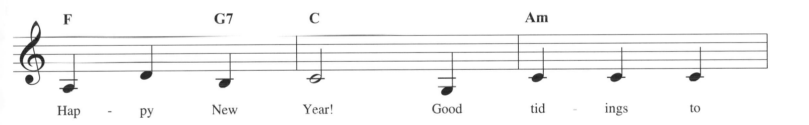

Hap - py New Year! Good tid - ings to

you, wher - ev - er you are. Good tid - ings for

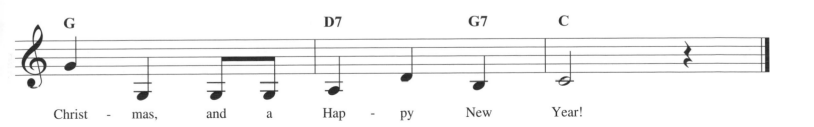

Christ - mas, and a Hap - py New Year!

WHAT ARE YOU DOING NEW YEAR'S EVE?

By FRANK LOESSER

Slowly and sentimentally

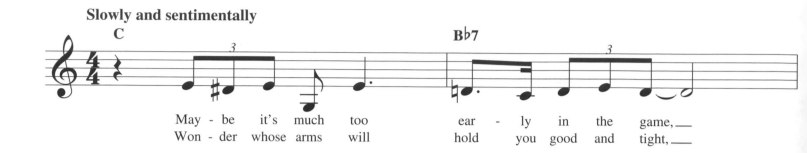

May - be it's much too ear - ly in the game, ___
Won - der whose arms will hold you good and tight, ___

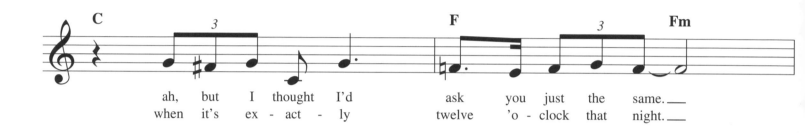

ah, but I thought I'd ask you just the same. ___
when it's ex - act - ly twelve 'o - clock that night. ___

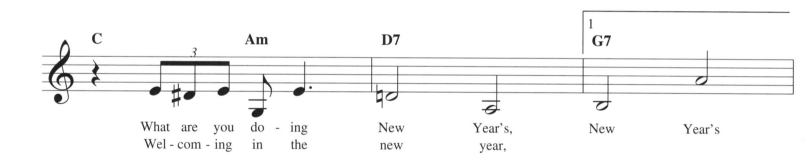

What are you do - ing the New Year's, New Year's
Wel - com - ing in the new new year,

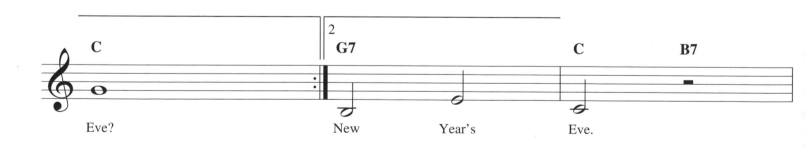

Eve? New Year's Eve.

May - be I'm cra - zy to sup - pose

I'd ev - er be the one you chose

out of the thou - sand in - vi - ta - tions

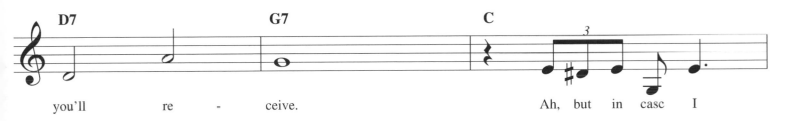

you'll re - ceive. Ah, but in case I

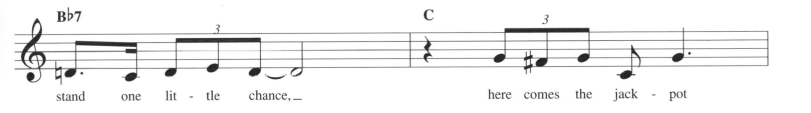

stand one lit - tle chance, __ here comes the jack - pot

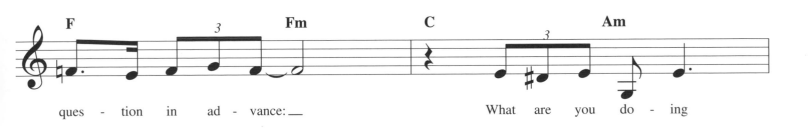

ques - tion in ad - vance: __ What are you do - ing

New Year's, New Year's Eve?

WHAT CHILD IS THIS?

Words by WILLIAM C. DIX
16th Century English Melody

WONDERFUL CHRISTMASTIME

Words and Music by
PAUL McCARTNEY

Moderately

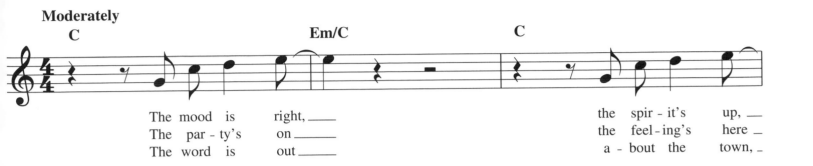

The mood is right, ____ the spir-it's up, __
The par-ty's on _____ the feel-ing's here __
The word is out _____ a-bout the town, __

____ we're here to-night __ and that's e-nough. __
____ that on-ly comes __ this time of year. __
____ to lift a glass, __ oh don't look down. __

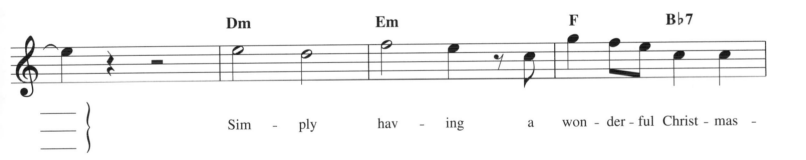

____ Sim - ply hav - ing a won-der-ful Christ-mas-

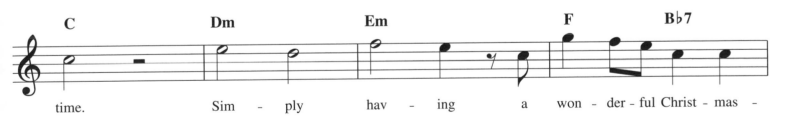

time. Sim - ply hav - ing a won-der-ful Christ-mas-

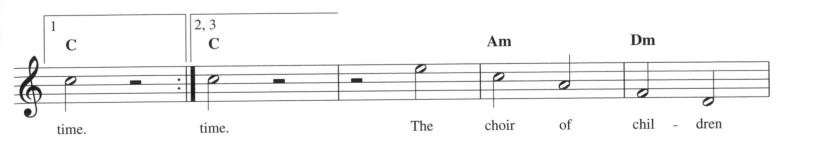

time.   time.   The choir of chil-dren

152

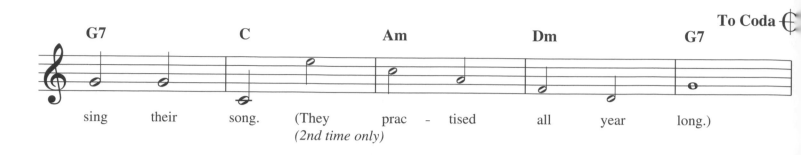

sing   their   song.   (They   prac - tised   all   year   long.)
(2nd time only)

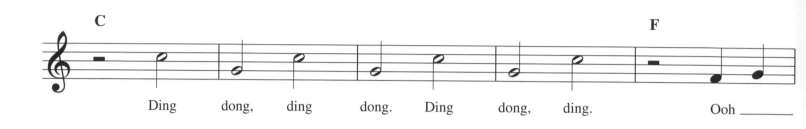

Ding   dong,   ding   dong.   Ding   dong,   ding.   Ooh _____

_____   Ooh _____

Do do   do   do   do do do   We're

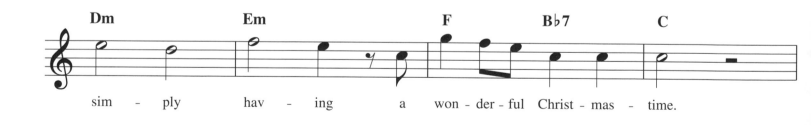

sim – ply   hav – ing   a   won - der - ful   Christ - mas - time.

Sim – ply   hav – ing   a   won - der - ful   Christ - mas - time.

CODA

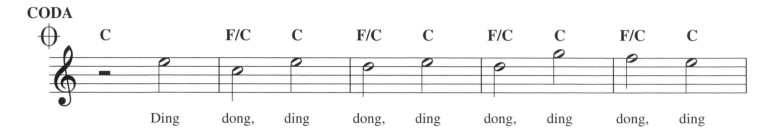

Ding   dong,   ding   dong,   ding   dong,   ding   dong,   ding

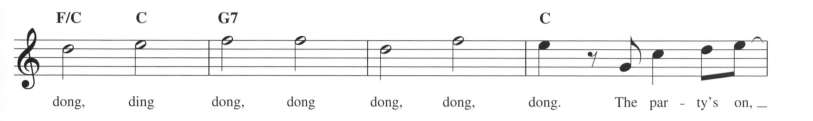

dong,   ding   dong,   dong   dong,   dong,   dong.   The par - ty's on, __

__   the spir - it's   up, _____

we're here   to - night ____   and that's   e - nough. _

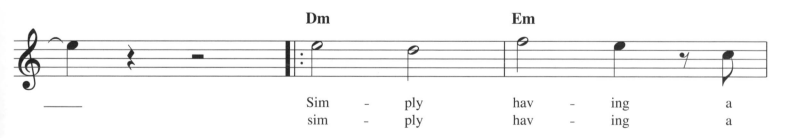

_____   Sim - ply   hav - ing   a
            sim - ply   hav - ing   a

won - der - ful Christ - mas - time.   We're
won - der - ful Christ - mas -   time.

YOU'RE ALL I WANT FOR CHRISTMAS

Words and Music by GLEN MOORE
and SEGER ELLIS

Moderately

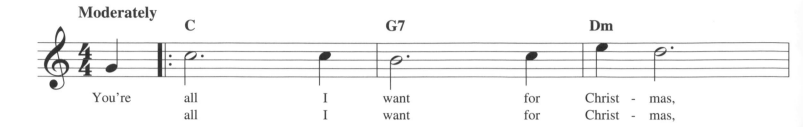

You're   all   I   want   for   Christ - mas,
all   I   want   for   Christ - mas,

all   I   want   my   whole   life   through._____
and   if   all   my   dreams   come   true,_____

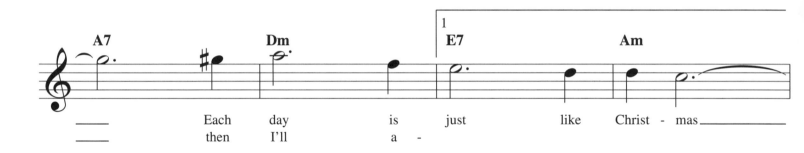

_____   Each   day   is   just   like   Christ - mas_____
_____   then   I'll   a -

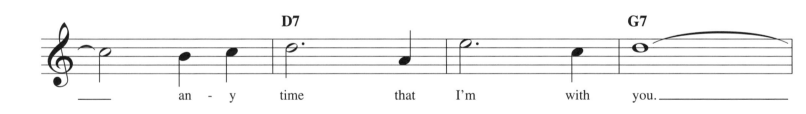

_____   an - y   time   that   I'm   with   you._____

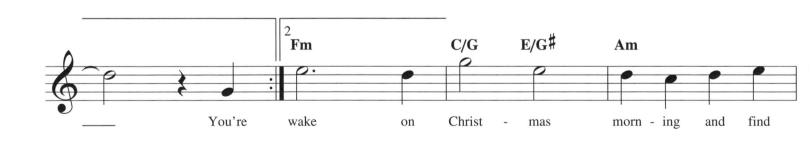

_____   You're   wake   on   Christ - mas   morn - ing   and   find

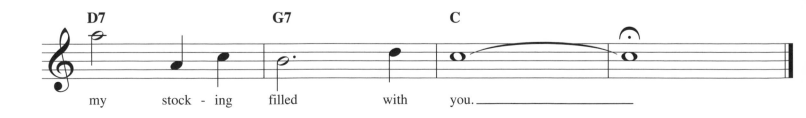

my   stock - ing   filled   with   you._____

CHORD SPELLER

C chords

C	C–E–G
Cm	C–Eb–G
C7	C–E–G–Bb
Cdim	C–Eb–Gb
C+	C–E–G#

C# or Db chords

C#	C#–F–G#
C#m	C#–E–G#
C#7	C#–F–G#–B
C#dim	C#–E–G
C#+	C#–F–A

D chords

D	D–F#–A
Dm	D–F–A
D7	D–F#–A–C
Ddim	D–F–Ab
D+	D–F#–A#

Eb chords

Eb	Eb–G–Bb
Ebm	Eb–Gb–Bb
Eb7	Eb–G–Bb–Db
Ebdim	Eb–Gb–A
Eb+	Eb–G–B

E chords

E	E–G#–B
Em	E–G–B
E7	E–G#–B–D
Edim	E–G–Bb
E+	E–G#–C

F chords

F	F–A–C
Fm	F–Ab–C
F7	F–A–C–Eb
Fdim	F–Ab–B
F+	F–A–C#

F# or Gb chords

F#	F#–A#–C#
F#m	F#–A–C#
F#7	F#–A#–C#–E
F#dim	F#–A–C
F#+	F#–A#–D

G chords

G	G–B–D
Gm	G–Bb–D
G7	G–B–D–F
Gdim	G–Bb–Db
G+	G–B–D#

G# or Ab chords

Ab	Ab–C–Eb
Abm	Ab–B–Eb
Ab7	Ab–C–Eb–Gb
Abdim	Ab–B–D
Ab+	Ab–C–E

A chords

A	A–C#–E
Am	A–C–E
A7	A–C#–E–G
Adim	A–C–Eb
A+	A–C#–F

Bb chords

Bb	Bb–D–F
Bbm	Bb–Db–F
Bb7	Bb–D–F–Ab
Bbdim	Bb–Db–E
Bb+	Bb–D–F#

B chords

B	B–D#–F#
Bm	B–D–F#
B7	B–D#–F#–A
Bdim	B–D–F
B+	B–D#–G

Important Note: A slash chord (C/E, G/B) tells you that a certain bass note is to be played under a particular harmony. In the case of C/E, the chord is C and the bass note is E.

HAL LEONARD PRESENTS
FAKE BOOKS FOR BEGINNERS!

Entry-level fake books! These books feature larger-than-most fake book notation with simplified harmonies and melodies – and all songs are in the key of C. An introduction addresses basic instruction in playing from a fake book.

YOUR FIRST FAKE BOOK
00240112.................................$19.95

THE EASY FAKE BOOK
00240144.................................$19.95

THE SIMPLIFIED FAKE BOOK
00240168.................................$19.95

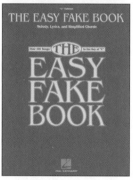

THE BEATLES EASY FAKE BOOK
00240309.................................$19.95

THE EASY BROADWAY FAKE BOOK
00240180.................................$19.95

THE EASY CHRISTMAS FAKE BOOK – 2ND EDITION
00240209.................................$19.95

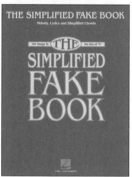

THE EASY CLASSICAL FAKE BOOK
00240262.................................$19.95

THE EASY CONTEMPORARY CHRISTIAN FAKE BOOK
00240328.................................$19.95

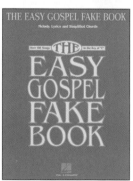

THE EASY GOSPEL FAKE BOOK
00240169.................................$19.95

THE EASY HYMN FAKE BOOK
00240207.................................$19.95

THE EASY MOVIE FAKE BOOK
00240295.................................$19.95

THE EASY SHOW TUNES FAKE BOOK
00240297.................................$19.95

THE EASY STANDARDS FAKE BOOK
00240294.................................$19.95

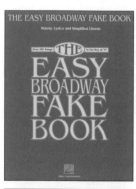

THE EASY WORSHIP FAKE BOOK
00240265.................................$19.95

THE EASY FORTIES FAKE BOOK
00240252.................................$19.95

MORE OF THE EASY FORTIES FAKE BOOK
00240287.................................$19.95

THE EASY FIFTIES FAKE BOOK
00240255.................................$19.95

MORE OF THE EASY FIFTIES FAKE BOOK
00240288.................................$19.95

THE EASY SIXTIES FAKE BOOK
00240253.................................$19.95

MORE OF THE EASY SIXTIES FAKE BOOK
00240289.................................$19.95

THE EASY SEVENTIES FAKE BOOK
00240256.................................$19.95

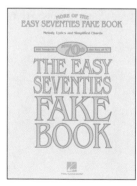

MORE OF THE EASY SEVENTIES FAKE BOOK
00240290.................................$19.95

Prices, contents and availability subject to change without notice.

FOR MORE INFORMATION, SEE YOUR LOCAL MUSIC DEALER, OR WRITE TO:

HAL•LEONARD®
CORPORATION

7777 W. BLUEMOUND RD. P.O. BOX 13819 MILWAUKEE, WI 53213

www.halleonard.com

0608

Christmas Collections
from Hal Leonard
All books arranged for piano, voice & guitar.

All-Time Christmas Favorites – Second Edition
This second edition features an all-star lineup of 32 Christmas classics, including: Blue Christmas • The Chipmunk Song • The Christmas Song • Frosty the Snow Man • Here Comes Santa Claus • I Saw Mommy Kissing Santa Claus • Jingle-Bell Rock • Let It Snow! Let It Snow! Let It Snow! • Merry Christmas, Darling • Nuttin' for Christmas • Rockin' Around the Christmas Tree • Rudolph the Red-Nosed Reindeer • Santa, Bring My Baby Back (To Me) • There Is No Christmas like a Home Christmas • and more.
00359051 ....$10.95

The Best Christmas Songs Ever – 4th Edition
69 all-time favorites are included in the 4th edition of this collection of Christmas tunes. Includes: Auld Lang Syne • Coventry Carol • Frosty the Snow Man • Happy Holiday • It Came Upon the Midnight Clear • O Holy Night • Rudolph the Red-Nosed Reindeer • Silver Bells • What Child Is This? • and many more.
00359130 ....$19.95

The Big Book of Christmas Songs
An outstanding collection of over 120 all-time Christmas favorites and hard-to-find classics. Features: Angels We Have Heard on High • As Each Happy Christmas • Auld Lang Syne • The Boar's Head Carol • Christ Was Born on Christmas Day • Bring a Torch Jeannette, Isabella • Carol of the Bells • Coventry Carol • Deck the Halls • The First Noel • The Friendly Beasts • God Rest Ye Merry Gentlemen • I Heard the Bells on Christmas Day • It Came Upon a Midnight Clear • Jesu, Joy of Man's Desiring • Joy to the World • Masters in This Hall • O Holy Night • The Story of the Shepherd • 'Twas the Night Before Christmas • What Child Is This? • and many more. Includes guitar chord frames.
00311520 ....$19.95

Christmas Songs – Budget Books
Save some money this Christmas with this fabulous budget-priced collection of 100 holiday favorites: All I Want for Christmas Is You • Christmas Time Is Here • Feliz Navidad • Grandma Got Run Over by a Reindeer • Happy Holiday • I'll Be Home for Christmas • Jesus Born on This Day • Last Christmas • Merry Christmas, Baby • O Holy Night • Please Come Home for Christmas • Rockin' Around the Christmas Tree • Some Children See Him • We Need a Little Christmas • What Child Is This? • and more.
00310887 ....$12.95

The Definitive Christmas Collection – 3rd Edition
Revised with even more Christmas classics, this must-have 3rd edition contains 127 top songs, such as: Blue Christmas • Christmas Time Is Here • Do You Hear What I Hear • The First Noel • A Holly Jolly Christmas • Jingle-Bell Rock • Little Saint Nick • Merry Christmas, Darling • O Holy Night • Rudolph, the Red-Nosed Reindeer • Silver and Gold • We Need a Little Christmas • You're All I Want for Christmas • and more!
00311602 ....$24.95

Essential Songs – Christmas
Over 100 essential holiday favorites: Blue Christmas • The Christmas Song • Deck the Hall • Frosty the Snow Man • A Holly Jolly Christmas • I'll Be Home for Christmas • Joy to the World • Let It Snow! Let It Snow! Let It Snow! • My Favorite Things • Rudolph the Red-Nosed Reindeer • Silver Bells • and more!
00311241 ....$24.95

Happy Holidays
50 favorite songs of the holiday season, including: Baby, It's Cold Outside • The Christmas Shoes • Emmanuel • The First Chanukah Night • The Gift • Happy Holiday • I Yust Go Nuts at Christmas • The Most Wonderful Time of the Year • Silver Bells • Who Would Imagine a King • Wonderful Christmastime • and more.
00310909 ....$16.95

Tim Burton's The Nightmare Before Christmas
This book features 11 songs from Tim Burton's creepy animated classic, with music and lyrics by Danny Elfman. Songs include: Jack's Lament • Jack's Obsession • Kidnap the Sandy Claws • Making Christmas • Oogie Boogie's Song • Poor Jack • Sally's Song • This Is Halloween • Town Meeting Song • What's This? • Finale/Reprise.
00312488 ....$12.95

Ultimate Christmas – 3rd Edition
100 seasonal favorites: Auld Lang Syne • Bring a Torch, Jeannette, Isabella • Carol of the Bells • The Chipmunk Song • Christmas Time Is Here • The First Noel • Frosty the Snow Man • Gesù Bambino • Happy Holiday • Happy Xmas (War Is Over) • Hymne • Jesu, Joy of Man's Desiring • Jingle-Bell Rock • March of the Toys • My Favorite Things • The Night Before Christmas Song • Pretty Paper • Silver and Gold • Silver Bells • Suzy Snowflake • What Child Is This • The Wonderful World of Christmas • and more.
00361399 ....$19.95